eroon
ganda
Yemen
Ethiopia
Kenya
Tanzania
Burundi
vanda
Madagascar
India
Sumatra
Java
Bali
Vietnam
Borneo
Celebes
Flores
Timor
Papua
New Guinea

# Coffee

# Coffee

## A
### Connoisseur's
### Companion

## CLAUDIA · RODEN

Illustrated by
**MURRAY ZANONI**

**RANDOM HOUSE**
**NEW YORK**

To the memory of my parents, Cesar and Nelly Douek,
and my brother Zaki

Published in the United Kingdom by
Pavilion Books Limited, London.
First published in 1977 by Faber and Faber Limited.

Library of Congress Cataloging-in-Publication Data
Roden, Claudia.
    Coffee: a connoisseur's companion / Claudia Roden:
illustrated by Murray Zanoni. – Rev. and expanded ed.
        p.   cm.
    Includes index.
    ISBN 0-679-43739-8
    1. Coffee.   2. Cookery (Coffee)   I. Title.
    TX415.R62  1995    94-18119
    641.3'373 – dc20

Designed by Janet James

Manufactured in Singapore.

24689753

First U.S. Edition

# Contents

# Introduction

I have loved coffee ever since, as young children in Cairo, we waited outside my parents' bedroom door for signs of their awakening. When the shadows on the frosted glass began to move, a signal and an invitation to come in, we pounced and raced for the coveted places in the large double bed where we waited for the coffee ritual to start.

Maria, our Yugoslav nanny and housekeeper, brought in a large brass tray ornately engraved in praise of Allah, on which were placed five small cups in delicate bone china with gold arabesques near the rim. A

glass of water held a piece of ice chipped from the block in the ice box, and was scented with a drop of orange flower water. A small plate carried a pile of oriental petits fours filled with dates, pistachios or ground almonds. My father poured out the coffee from two small copper *kanakas* (or *ibriks* as they are called in Turkish) with much ceremony, carefully shaking his hand so as to drop a little of the much prized froth in each cup. We passed the water round, then drank the syrupy black brew in little sips and with much reverence.

In Egypt, no one thought children should not drink coffee. It was usually assumed that we would like it sweet, and it was made accordingly and served with home-made preserves and jams. When we had finished, we turned over the tiny cups, for at least one member of the company was reputed to be good at fortune telling. Everything could be read in the grounds: travels, unexpected bequests, weddings.

My schooldays in France, as well as my more recent travels throughout Italy and many other countries to research their foods, have enabled me to enjoy coffee in different forms around the world.

In the seventeen years since the first edition of this book was published a great deal has happened in the world of coffee, though not quite so much in the traditional coffee-drinking countries of Europe and the Middle East where each country has continued with its own traditional ways. The greatest changes have been in Japan, a tea-drinking country which has adopted coffee in a very big way, and in America where something of a coffee revolution has taken place. There have been changes in the coffee trade, in the different producing countries and also in consumer trends. While the consumption of commercial coffees has gone down, the consumption of quality coffees has increased spectacularly. The interest in real premium quality coffees referred to as speciality coffees, and in America also as 'gourmet', 'fancy' and 'whole bean' coffees, has been phenomenal.

What has happened in America is something to marvel at. In a country where once coffee was drunk at all times of the day, including before and during lunch, but where it was impossible ever to get a drinkable cup, you now get exquisite coffee. In the States there is a passionate dedication to quality and an evangelical zeal in the ever-expanding speciality trade. Among consumers there is also an extraordinary awareness of the culture of coffee – from interest in the country of origin and knowledge of production methods and the lives of plantation workers to appreciation of the roaster's art and familiarity with the taste of different beans. The coffee revolution has followed the food revolution. Both are seen as a Europeanization of American habits based on a sensual perception of taste. The interest is limited to a minority but it is a young and ever-growing minority.

America has fallen in love with coffee. It has its purists and fundamentalists, evangelists and proselytizers. In most cities, and in some cases in every neighbourhood, there are speciality coffee stores and coffee houses offering excellent coffee. There are coffee festivals and seminars, courses on roasting, grinding and brewing, coffee tastings, tours to coffee plantations and magazines devoted to coffee. The affair with coffee is following various trends, some of them controversial and the subject of passionate debate. Most importantly it takes the form of 'espresso mania'. In Seattle, the new coffee capital at the forefront of the trend, there is the extraordinary phenomenon of moveable espresso carts on street corners, in shopping malls, bookshops and seemingly everywhere. One ever-growing trend decried by purists is for 'flavoured' coffees, and the merits and health risks of the processes involved in making decaffeinated coffees are also a subject of controversy.

In Britain there has been an improvement in the coffee served in public places, and the specialist coffee trade is finding a growing clientele, but it is small in comparison to America. All over the world, and especially in America, the 'gourmet' sector is the growth area with an ever greater number of consumers. The best coffees are in demand. Even commercial brand roasters have upgraded their coffees. In response to demand and appreciation, the producers of top-quality coffees have maintained their quality and identity and their high standards, while the general medium-quality coffees have deteriorated because they have become less profitable and the incentive is not there to keep up the standard.

This book is basically the same in structure as when it first came out. I have expanded on new developments and have gone into more depth in areas where interest has grown. I have also added my voice to the debates and controversies. It is basically for coffee-lovers – for beginners as well as for connoisseurs. It is about how to make perfect coffee and about the infinite possibilities to be explored. I have included early legends of exotic beginnings and brief moments of social history as well as aspects of the coffee trade and its cultivation, including the coffee tree and methods of production. The lore of coffee is as fascinating as the lore of wine and it is as important to know for a fuller appreciation of the drink.

Few beverages are as intoxicating, heartwarming and utterly pleasurable as really good coffee. Flavour, body, colour, stimulation and above all aroma play their part in making it so. It is not surprising that it is firmly established as one of the essential pleasures of our life today.

# One

# History

# History

## A Tumultuous Start

Coffee is only three centuries old for us in the West, and not one bean was made to germinate outside Africa and Arabia before the seventeenth century. Then, coming from the Levant and arriving first in Venice, it swept tumultuously through the towns of Europe and into America, changing the style of life as it went. The propagation of the plant followed in each European country's colonies in what was often a series of chance adventures.

It acquired its name from the Arabic *qahwah*, through its Turkish form *kahveh* becoming *café* in French, *caffè* in Italian, *koffie* in Dutch and *Kaffee* in German.

Originally a poetic name for wine, the word was transferred towards the end of the thirteenth century in the Yemen to a drink made from the berry of the coffee tree. One explanation for this is that coffee, first inaugurated in Sufi mystic circles, had come to replace the forbidden wine as a drink during religious ceremonies. Delighted by the wakefulness the new drink produced and the help it gave them in their nightly prayers, the early Mohammedans honoured it by giving it the poetic endearment with which they had sung the praise of wine.

Although the earliest written mention of coffee was by Rhazes, an Arabian physician in the tenth century, cultivation may have begun as early as A.D. 575. The coffee tree of the *Coffea arabica* species which gives the best quality coffee is indigenous to Ethiopia, where it grows wild. Other species, such as the *robusta* and the *liberica*, have since been found in other parts of Africa. *Arabica* was first cultivated in the Arabian colony of Harar in Ethiopia. Intensive cultivation came only in the fifteenth century in the Yemen area of South Arabia, from seedlings brought from Ethiopia.

Early legends ascribe the discovery of coffee to various people. The favourite one which has been generally adopted is that of the 'dancing goats'. Kaldi, a young Abyssinian goatherd, used to his sleepy goats, noticed to his amazement that after chewing certain berries they began to prance about excitedly. He tried the berries himself, forgot his troubles, lost his heavy heart and became the happiest person in 'happy Arabia'. A monk from a nearby monastery surprised Kaldi in this state, decided to try the berries too, and invited his brothers to join him. They all felt more alert that night during their prayers. Soon all the monks of the realm were chewing the berries and praying without feeling drowsy.

Another popular tradition of which I am personally fond is related by a certain Hadjiji Khalifa. It concerns Ali bin Omar al-Shadhili, the saint of al-Mukha. Charged with misconduct with the king's daughter who was staying with him for a cure, he was banished into the mountains of Wusab in the Yemen. He and his disciples who followed him in exile ate the berries and drank the decoction they made from boiling them. Then, it seems, victims of an itch epidemic which plagued the inhabitants of

Mukha came to him and were cured by taking his coffee. This won him an honourable return and gave him the position of patron saint of coffee growers, coffee-house keepers and coffee drinkers. In Algeria, coffee is also knows as 'shadhiliye' after him.

Coffee berries were eaten whole at first, or crushed and mixed with fat. Later, a kind of wine was made with the fermented pulp. In about A.D. 1000 a decoction was made of the dried fruit, beans, hull and all. The practice of roasting the beans was started around the thirteenth century. The drink became popular with dervishes and spread to Mecca and Medina. By the end of the fifteenth century it was passed on by Muslim pilgrims to all parts of the Islamic world, as far as Persia, Egypt, Turkey and North Africa, providing Arabia with a most profitable trade.

Houses of the wealthy had a special room used only for drinking coffee, and servants employed solely to make it. Coffee houses sprang up everywhere people congregated. The more they frequented the coffee houses, the less they went to the mosques. Backgammon, mankala, dancing, music and singing, activities frowned on by the stricter adherents of Islam, also went on in the coffee houses. Having made a start within religion, coffee became a threat to religious observance. The pious tried to prohibit it by invoking the law proscribing wine-drinking.

The establishment, too, was afraid of the joy of life and sense of freedom liberated in the coffee drinkers. Coffee became a subversive drink, gathering people together and sharpening their wits, encouraging political arguments and revolt – a characteristic which was to follow it into

Europe and which was felt particularly in times of social unrest. Coffee houses were to be charged again and again with immorality and vice, whether in Cairo, Mecca or Constantinople. At the instigation of religious fanatics or at the whim of a Bey, a Pasha or Kadi (but also once for the sake of a favourite courtesan) they were mobbed and wrecked.

Of the sporadic persecution of coffee houses and drinkers, the most savage was in 1656 when the Ottoman Grand Vizir Koprili suppressed the coffee houses for political reasons, and prohibited coffee. For a first violation the punishment was cudgelling. For a second, the offender was put into a leather bag, which was sewn up and thrown into the Bosphorus. The straits thus claimed many a man.

The introduction of coffee into Europe was not without pitfalls. The more avid its adoption and the wider it spread, the more hostility it aroused. A *Women's Petition Against Coffee* was published in London in 1674, complaining that men were never to be found at home during times of domestic crisis since they were always in the coffee houses, and that the drink rendered them impotent. The following year, in France, attempts were made to discredit the drink, which was seen as an unwelcome competitor by the wine merchants.

In Italy it was the priests who appealed to Pope Clement VIII to have the use of coffee forbidden among Christians. Satan, they said, had forbidden his followers, the infidel Moslems, the use of wine because it was used in the Holy Communion, and given them instead his 'hellish black brew'. It seems the Pope liked the drink, for his reply was: 'Why, this Satan's drink is so delicious that it would be a pity to let the infidels have exclusive use of it. We shall cheat Satan by baptizing it.' Thus coffee was declared a truly Christian beverage by a farsighted Pope. However, this did not stop the Council of Ten in Venice from trying to eradicate the 'social cankers', the *caffès*, which they charged with immorality, vice and corruption.

Coffee also met with opposition in Sweden, Prussia and Hanover. Frederick the Great, annoyed with the great sums of money going to foreign coffee merchants, issued the following declaration in 1777:

'It is disgusting to note the increase in the quantity of coffee used by my subjects and the amount of money that goes out of the country in consequence. Everybody is using coffee. If possible

# History

this must be prevented. My people must drink beer. His Majesty was brought up on beer, and so were his officers. Many battles have been fought and won by soldiers nourished on beer; and the King does not believe that coffee-drinking soldiers can be depended upon to endure hardships or to beat his enemies in case of the occurrence of another war.'

It must be said that with all the official sanctions and taxation and the threats of disease and persecution, prohibitions were always more honoured in the breach than in the observance. In fact, coffee gained a greater impetus from the notoriety, and coffee houses survived every effort to suppress them.

## Three Hundred Years of Trade

An Italian wrote from Constantinople in 1615:

> 'The Turks have a drink of black colour, which during the summer is very cooling, whereas in the winter it heats and warms the body, remaining always the same beverage and not changing its substance. They swallow it hot as it comes from the fire and they drink it in long draughts, not at dinner time, but as a kind of dainty and sipped slowly while talking with one's friends. One cannot find any meetings among them where they drink it not . . . With this drink which they call "cahue", they divert themselves in their conversations . . . When I return I will bring some with me and I will impart the knowledge to the Italians.'

Many European travellers to the Levant were already reporting on the strange drink. In the same year Venetian merchants brought coffee beans into Europe from Moka, five years after the Dutch brought tea, and eighty years after cocoa was introduced by the Spanish.

This was the start of a most lucrative trade for the Arabians, one they jealously guarded for a hundred years while they were the sole providers of coffee to the world. Berries were not allowed out of the country without first being steeped in boiling water or parched to destroy their power of germination and strangers were prohibited from visiting plantations – a difficult task with so many pilgrims journeying to Mecca. It was in fact a pilgrim from India who smuggled out the first beans capable of germination.

The first coffee plant to be brought to Europe was stolen by Dutch traders in 1616. The Netherlands East India Company realized the commercial advantages of cultivating the bean and by the end of the century they had set up plantations in the Dutch colonies of Ceylon, Java and Sumatra, Celebes, Timor and Bali.

The French followed in a less businesslike, more romantic way with the introduction of coffee into their own colonies. A coffee plant was presented to Louis XIV by the burgomaster of Amsterdam in 1714. It blossomed in the Jardin des Plantes, tended by the royal botanist, Antoine de Jussieu. It was destined, through the initiative of a young naval officer from Normandy, Gabriel Mathieu de Clieu, to become the progenitor of all the coffees of the Caribbean and the Americas. Delighted by the drink he discovered in the Paris coffee houses during a visit from Martinique, and hearing about the plantations in Java, he became obsessed with the idea of starting cultivation in the French colonies.

Having obtained a seedling through clever intrigue, he set sail for Martinique with the tender young plant in a glass box. The voyage was fraught with misadventure and the plant was in constant danger, not least from a passenger who repeatedly tried to destroy it and even managed to tear off some leaves during a struggle with de Clieu. Surviving a fierce tempest and flooding with salt water as well as a period of water rationing during which it shared de Clieu's own scant supply, the seedling was eventually planted in the officer's garden in Martinique, surrounded by thorny bushes and under constant surveillance of an armed guard. This tiny plant was to provide all the rich estates of the West Indies and Latin America.

Coffee was introduced soon after in Spain's West Indian Colonies of Puerto Rico and Cuba.

Britain was the last country to cultivate coffee in its colonies. It started cultivation in Jamaica in 1730 and waited till 1840 to begin cultivation in India, where it had previously concentrated on tea.

At the same time Brazil entered the field, acquiring the plant, as legend relates, through the charms of a lieutenant colonel Francisco de Melo Palheta. The Brazilian officer, having attracted the attentions of the Governor's wife on a visit to French Guiana in 1727, received a coffee plant hidden in a bouquet of flowers as a token of her affection. This gift was the start of the greatest coffee empire in the world. Progress was slow at first, with Roman Catholic missionaries playing a major part in spreading coffee growing throughout Brazil and in other parts of South America.

In the middle of the nineteenth century, the terrible leaf disease *Hemileia vastatrix* struck Asia. Within a few years it had completely wiped out coffee in India and Ceylon, Java, Sumatra and Malaya, leaving the field wide open to Brazil with its ideal volcanic soil, its moist foggy climate and its large slave labour force.

By the end of the century Brazil had achieved supremacy in world coffee production, a position it still holds today. The mass consumption of coffee had spread throughout the world, and coffee had entered its golden age. It is Brazil's growing and enormous production that has changed the role of coffee from luxury drink to common everyday beverage. Its problem soon became one of over-planting and over-production, while in Colombia, it was a matter of overcoming the difficulties of growing and transportation on the high slopes of the Andes.

So large and dependable has the world consumer demand become, with America, which takes about one third of the world's supply, in the lead, that to satisfy it a coffee growing belt has spread to all lands of suitable climate across the world. Lying between the tropic of Cancer and the tropic of Capricorn, the belt spreads thickly across the Americas, through the islands of the Caribbean and the now turbulent areas of Africa and Arabia. It embraces the Malgasy Republic, India and the East Indian and Pacific Islands. In more than sixty countries, it provides a living for some 25 million people and gives the beans a most important part in world trade as a commodity second only to oil.

Since the Second World War the main feature of world coffee production and commerce has been the enormous rise in importance of the African countries as coffee suppliers. Their contribution has been mainly in the cheaper coffees in competition with Brazil.

Brazil, however, with Colombia a close second, still dominates the coffee markets of the world. While Yemen, the first producer, slips into relative inactivity, some of the old coffee producing countries are making inroads into the South American supremacy.

Despite its success, the history of coffee production has been the chequered one of a delicate tropical crop threatened by the vagaries of weather, disease and natural disaster. With the growing fierce competition of the last decades, it has also been one of recurring cycles of over-production and under-production with the accompanying price changes. Merchandizing developed into a ruthless free-for-all, with price cutting and dumping and burning of mountains of unsaleable coffee (as in Brazil) for many years. The devastating Black Frost, which crippled millions of trees in Brazil on the night of 17th July 1975, and the political unrest in many African countries, contributed with Brazil's crop tragedy to a temporary world shortage and great price rises.

In the 1950s producing countries attempted to stabilize production levels and prices through short-term agreements between themselves. In 1962 the first long-term International Coffee Agreement took place at the United Nations in New York. Three other agreements followed to balance the supply and demand for coffee, to ensure a fair price structure and to encourage co-operation between exporting and importing countries. The Agreements have been administered in London by the International Coffee Organisation. They have had a stabilizing effect through setting a price range for coffee through a system of adjustable export quotas. But the last agreement expired in 1989.

With obvious conflicts of interest, growing dissension on quotas, selectivity and readjustment systems and criticism that prices were kept down for the consuming countries, the producing countries failed to agree to renew the system. The market is now free and there are no quotas. The result has been disastrous for the producing countries, whose economies lie precariously on the fortunes of the coffee crop. Oversupply caused prices to tumble by half. Consuming countries, and particularly the United States, have benefited from the free market. Producers desperately need the co-operation of consumers in establishing an instrument to regulate the market and defend their prices. But the large roasting firms which control the American market want a market-orientated agreement. However, they have found that although an increase in prices slows down consumption, a decrease in prices does not have the opposite effect.

The more well-known top-quality coffees have maintained their identity and appreciation, and still find a market. It is the demand for medium type coffees that has suffered. Because they are less profitable, many growers have abandoned them. Colombia and Peru have suffered the effects of the narcotics trade; a fall in the earnings of coffee growers has worsened the problem. Many farmers have turned instead to growing coca for cocaine.

Merchants are to some extent protected against price changes in the 'futures' market by buying and selling in advance. The Coffee Terminal Market Association acts mostly as an international insurance market, interpreting world conditions and anticipating supply and demand trends. Speculation, however, also results in artificial price rises.

Trading for the cheaper *robusta* coffees alone is carried on at the London Commodity Exchange, at 1 Commodity Quay, St Katharine Docks, while the futures market for *arabicas* is the New York Coffee and Sugar Exchange. Quality Milds and Brazils – especially those in the private sector – are sold straight to the buyers.

# Coffee Houses

Although their history has not been smooth, various styles of coffee houses have developed throughout the world for the specific purpose of drinking this privileged brew. We have the leisurely Continental sidewalk cafés and the *cafés concerts* for the family outing. There are the German *Kaffeeklatsch* ('coffee and gossip') gardens where people bring their own cakes and sandwiches, and the American coffee bars where customers have only a few minutes to snatch a cup of coffee sitting on a high stool.

A certain flavour and style are common to most. Inaugurated in the Levant, they captured the leisure and tranquillity of the local way of life. Coffee houses encourage the convivial spirit. People go there to chat and gossip and be entertained, and sometimes they go to read the newspaper and to play chess or backgammon. In most parts, especially around the Mediterranean, they are not pressed to order nor hurried to leave.

Catering equally for the working and the leisured classes, they have tended to be democratic in character. As a French periodical of the 1850s entitled *Le Café* pointed out in its slogan: 'The *salon* stood for privilege, the café stands for equality.' Coffee has been called the intellectual drink of democracy. In times of upheaval, coffee houses became revolutionary centres, encouraging the interchange of ideas and usually generating liberal and radical opinions. It has been said that the French Revolution was fomented in coffee-house meetings, and the Café Foy was the starting point of its mob spirit.

However, the democratic record had not always been sustained. Women were undemocratically barred from all coffee houses in England, and in the early days of coffee in Germany the drink was reserved by royal decree for the elect alone. In 1781 Frederick the Great forbade the roasting of coffee except in the courts and royal establishments. He made exceptions in the case of the nobility, the clergy, some government officials and his own officers. The *crème de la crème* were obliged to purchase the coffee at high prices directly from the state, but the common people had all their applications for coffee-roasting licences refused. Those who managed to obtain some beans and roasted them illegally were found out by 'coffee smellers' – spies paid to roam the streets in search of revealing smells coming out of windows – and heavily fined.

While coffee drinking has been linked with agitations for greater freedom, ironically, its production in the Dutch East Indies, the West Indies, Brazil and most other parts was dependent on the work of slaves or forced labour, and was the result of colonial exploitation.

The character of each coffee house has naturally reflected that of its frequenters. Kasters Niebuhr writes about early Syrian coffee houses in 'Descriptions of Arabia' (Amsterdam, 1774):

> 'Being the only theatres for the exercise of profane eloquence, poor scholars attend here to amuse the people. Select portions are read, e.g. the adventures of Rustan Sal, a Persian hero. Some aspire to the praise of invention, and compose tales and fables. They walk up and down as they recite, or assuming oratorial consequence, harangue upon subjects chosen by themselves.

'In one coffee house at Damascus an orator was regularly hired to tell his stories at a fixed hour; in other cases he was more directly dependent upon the taste of his hearers, as at the conclusion of his discourse, whether it had consisted of literary topics or of loose idle tales, he looked to the audience for a voluntary contribution.'

The wife of Shah Abbas appointed a *mullah* to sit every day in the more turbulent establishments of Isfahan in Persia. His job was to entertain all day with points of law, history and poetry. Seated high in an ornate chair, he would also tell jokes, sing and recount the romantic and nostalgic stories of famous lovers or the Arabian Nights. Thus political hotheads were ignored and controversial issues avoided. Coffee-house storytellers are becoming fashionable again in Iran today, though sometimes it is the ubiquitous television that has taken over the role on the raised chair.

Anyone who has been to Italy knows how much the *caffè* is part of the good life. The people that frequent them are little different from those who could be seen around the piazza in Carlo Goldoni's play *La Bottega di Caffè* (1750), though at this time coffee houses often also functioned as barbers' shops and gambling houses.

Venetian coffee was said to surpass all others and the Café Florian's was said to be the best in Venice. Perhaps the most celebrated coffee house in the world, Florian was opened by Floriano Francesconi in 1720, by which time all the shops in the Piazza San Marco had already established themselves as coffee houses with chairs spilling out into the centre of the Square, superseding the lemonade vendors, 'acquacedratraios', who had previously sold coffee. People from all classes frequented Florian, mostly to hear the latest gossip, and Signor Floriano helped in the exchange, for he 'long concentrated in himself a knowledge more varied and multifarious than that possessed by any individual before or since'. Today, although waitresses no longer fasten flowers in the gentlemen's buttonholes, violins still serenade the ladies.

The first person to sell coffee in Paris, an American called Pascal, sent young coffee waiters through the streets with coffee pots and oil heaters, shouting '*Café! Café!*' and offering *petits noirs*. The French bourgeoisie ignored the drink, preferring wines and spirits, and left the oriental-style coffee houses to the poorer classes. However, when the Café Procope was opened by François Procope in 1689, its spacious elegance, its subtle tapestries and large gilt mirrors, the marble tables, chandeliers and paintings made coffee respectable and fashionable.

François Procope started as a *limonadier* with a royal licence to sell spices, barley water and lemonade; but he gave pride of place to coffee. Being opposite the Comédie Française, he attracted actors, authors, dramatists and musicians. Among the many famous 'hommes de lettres' who were his patrons were Voltaire, Rousseau, Diderot and Beaumarchais, and during the days of the Revolution, Marat, Robespierre and Danton. Today it is still a marvellous café and restaurant, serving fine food at 13 rue de l'Ancienne Comédie.

By 1843 Paris had become one large café, with 3,000 establishments. The historian Michelet described coffee as 'the great event which created new customs, and even modified human temperament'. He ascribed to it the spontaneous flow of wit which was characteristic of the time. The French coffee shop ennobled the ways of its frequenters by inaugurating a reign of temperance and luring people away from the cabaret.

Today the institution is still one where everything is discussed and where people sharpen their wits in debate. It is especially so at the Mabillon, Les Deux Magots and Café de Flore at the Quartier Latin. Here, as at the Véry, les Trois Provençaux and the Café de Chartres of the Palais Royal, the cafés have gained in prestige and reputation what they might have lost financially from customers who spend too long over a cup of coffee.

Historic cafés are still thriving. The Café de la Paix still attracts people to the boulevard des Capucines, Café Durand brings them to the place de la Madeleine, and Voisin's and Mapinot are for the fashionable of the rue St Honoré. You should visit Tortoni, Café Riche, Maison Dorée and the Café Anglais in the boulevard des Italiens. And of course in Montmartre there are the Café Madrid and the Chat Noir, where painters used to leave canvases in exchange for food and drink. They have appeared in many an Impressionist work and are often used as galleries. One could go on for ever naming the cafés that have not changed in three centuries.

An old anecdote was told to me of a Viennese coffee house where a man had been occupying a seat for some hours. He got up and asked a neighbour: 'Could you please keep my seat while I nip home for a quick cup of coffee?'

A tourist in Vienna in the early eighteenth century wrote about the town which has been called the 'mother of cafés':

'The city of Vienna is filled with coffee houses, where the novelists or those who busy themselves with newspapers delight to meet, to read the gazettes and discuss their contents. Some of these houses have a better reputation than others because such "zeitung-doctors" (doctors in journalism) gather there to pass most unhesitating judgement on the weightiest events, and to surpass all others in their opinions concerning political matters and considerations. All this wins them such respect that many congregate there because of them, and to enrich their minds with inventions and foolishness which they immediately run through the city to bring to the ears of the said personalities.'

After a battering of two wars, Viennese coffee houses still serve delicious coffee with horns, crescents and doughnuts to their habitués, and their special character – including the bentwood chairs and marble tables, rococo mouldings, great mirrors and chandeliers, old prints and posters – has been transported by emigrés all over the world. For this reason, at least, we owe a special debt to Franz George Kolschitsky, interpreter for the Turkish Army in 1683, and patron saint of Viennese coffee lovers. The retreating Turkish armies left behind sacks of green coffee beans when they abandoned the siege of Vienna. Kolschitsky collected the sacks and prepared the beans as the Ottomans had done. He sold cups of coffee from door to door and, when his wartime bravery was rewarded by the municipality with a house, he turned it into a coffee house. It was to be the model for all the Viennese cafés that became world famous, as much for their *mélangés* and *schwarze* coffees and their delicious pastries as for the spirit of a grand epoch.

There was a time when the streets of London were so full of coffee houses that people were sure to find one at every corner, guided by the ubiquitous signs of a Turkish coffee pot or the Sultan's head. If a sign did not catch the eye a person had only to sniff the air for the aroma of roasting coffee. England, in fact, had the first coffee house in Europe. It was opened by a Jew from Turkey, a certain Jacob who, benefiting from Cromwell's generous policy towards his co-religionists, was allowed to settle in England. He opened a coffee house in 1650 at Oxford at the Angel in the parish of St Peter-in-the-East. The first coffee house in London was opened two years later by one Pasqua Rosée, said to be either Armenian or Greek, or both, who had come to England as a servant. He set up with the help of his master in St Michael's Alley in Cornhill.

Having heard from travellers and merchants to the East about the 'novelty drink', the English were eager to adopt it. One of the most important upholders of the 'Turkish renegade', as coffee was sometimes called, was Sir Henry Blunt, puritan abstainer and so-called 'father' of the English coffee houses.

The influence of coffee houses was enormous on the political, social, literary and commercial life of the times. They were the stage for political debate, fringe centres of education and the origin of certain newspapers. Insurance houses, merchant banks and the stock exchange began in coffee houses. Everything, it seems, went on in these establishments. Edward Robinson describes them in his excellent *The Early English Coffee House*, first published in 1893 (New edition, Dolphin Press, 1972).

Arriving with Puritan rule, an aid to temperance and antidote to alcoholism, halfway between the open tavern and the club, they were well suited to the social climate of the time. They provided a release from the gloomy strictness, but 'decency was never outraged' and it was 'cheaper far than wine'. You could 'for a penny or two spend two or three hours' and you would come out more sprightly than when you came in.

Their democratic character was much in favour. All classes could meet, and nobody was excluded who 'laid down his penny at the bar', especially if he was of 'amiable disposition and a wit'. That is, everybody apart from women, for women were firmly excluded. Macaulay describes the mixed company at Wills': 'earls in stars and garters, clergymen in cassocks, pert templars, sheepish lads from the Universities, translators and index-makers in ragged coats'.

Some coffee houses were frequented by one particular group and eventually almost 'every rank and profession and every shade of political opinion had its own headquarters'. The Rota coffee house was essentially a debating society for the dissemination of republican ideas. Tillyard's was royalist, as was the Grecian in London, which was the beginning of the Royal Society.

Coffee houses near colleges were called 'penny universities' since there, it was said, a man could 'pick up more useful knowledge than he could if applying himself to his book for a whole month'. The penny was the price of a coffee.

Having flourished during the Commonwealth and survived the Great Fire, coffee houses slipped into a new role with the Restoration. They became less democratic, more establishment, for the fashionable, the gay and the rich, reflecting the social and intellectual life and splendour of the time. *The Connoisseur* in 1754 described the Bedford, which was typical of the new Restoration style: 'This coffee house is every night crowded with many parts. Almost everyone you meet is a polite scholar and a wit. Jokes and *bons mots* are echoed from box to box; every branch of literature is critically examined, and the merit of every production of the press or performance of the theatres weighed and determined.'

Certain coffee houses in the city were the general mart of stock job-
bers and brokers. One in Sweetings Alley became known as the Stock
Exchange coffee house. From some evolved the great Mercantile and
Shipping Exchange. A 'coffee man', Edward Lloyd, opened Lloyd's coffee house for seafaring men in Tower Street; here underwriters met over
coffee and listened to the gossip of the ships and the sea. Merchants and
shipowners came to insure their ships and their cargoes, and slaves were
occasionally bought. The Baltic Mercantile and Shipping Exchange
started at the Virginia and the Jerusalem.

Goldsmiths' and bankers' clerks would meet at coffee houses to settle
payments and do their 'outside business'. In 1682 the Bank of Credit
was formed and announced that they were ready to do business in the
coffee houses and that 'all persons that are desirous to subscribe may
come either to Garaway's, Jonathan's or the Amsterdam within Temple
Bar, Peter's Coffee House in Covent Garden, or the Mail Coffee House
at Charing Cross, at all of which places books will be ready and persons
attend from ten to twelve in the morning and from five to seven in the
evening'. A room was rented for the clerks to meet regularly at the Five
Bells. They later transferred to the Clearing House. At Tom's, the oldest
fire insurance service, called the Hand-in-Hand, was formed; this was
later incorporated in the Commercial Union. Even doctors used city
coffee houses as consulting rooms.

The gossip of the coffee houses
found expression in 'Newsletters'
privately commissioned by
wealthy individuals or
institutions such as the
Church. These handwritten
contributions gathered
from rumour were the most
valuable source of information
at a time when official newspapers
were heavily censored. Coffee houses also offered information as well as
a ready circulation for established newspapers such as the *Tatler*, the
*Spectator* and the *Guardian*.

Some provided a 'brass plate' or an ivory tablet with a pencil attached
for their customers to write their remarks. The items of news were

collected twice a day while still 'hot' for immediate entry. At Button's, a box in the shape of a lion's head awaited contributions for the *Guardian*.

However, the importance of coffee houses was not to last for ever. Their phenomenal rise was equalled only by their spectacular decline. When the time came they disappeared as quickly as they had come. They had served their unique social purpose and were no longer needed. Perhaps the English were unable to lay aside their traditional reserve for ever, at least without resorting to a genuinely intoxicating beverage. Not all the 'undesirables' could be eased out, and people did not like to find at their table 'a gripping Usurer, and next to him a gallant Furioso, then nigh to him a Virtuoso . . . a player . . . a Country Clown, some pragmatic . . . a sly phanatick . . . from all parts of the Earth; Dutch, Danes, Turks and Jews.' They were warned: 'If there you should observe a person without previous acquaintance, paying you extraordinary marks of civility, if he put in for a share of your conversation with a pretended air of deference; if he tenders his assistance, and would be suddenly thought your friend, avoid him as a pest; for these are the usual baits by which the unwary are caught.'

By the end of the eighteenth century the coffee houses, of which there had been thousands, had all disappeared. Most of them had become select members' clubs. The poor and the less exclusive had slipped back into their earlier rôle of taverns and chop houses. One institution was certainly pleased. The British East India Company, far behind the Dutch and the French in the cultivation of coffee in the British colonies, was more interested in selling tea. The British Government, wishing to improve trade with India and China, was glad of the opportunity to encourage tea drinking. Tea had already been adopted by the Royal Family and the Court, and women could at last join the men in the new and fashionable tea gardens. Tea was also better made.

The 'bitter black drink', as Pepys used to call coffee, was made in various ways, all equally peculiar. Usually served black, it was boiled with egg shells and sometimes mixed with mustard or sugar candy. Some concoctions included 'oatmeal, a pint of ale or any wine, ginger, honey or sugar to please the taste . . . butter might be added and any cordial powder or pleasant spice'. No wonder coffee was so easily dismissed from favour. Its popularity lay more in the realm of social history than in that of gastronomy.

It was only in the 1950s that coffee bars mushroomed again in Britain. The espresso coffee machine, invented by the Italian Achille Gaggia, in 1946, became the success story of the fifties. It was responsible for the rash of coffee bars which started in Soho and spread throughout the country. Young people could meet casually over a cup of coffee in a contemporary décor, which then meant tiles, wickerwork, bare bricks and matting. The style was exotic with tropical vegetation, homely and rustic with bunches of onions and garlic, or Italian with fleets of gondolas and Chianti bottles holding candles – a real departure from the old snack-bars of England. Pottery-makers and glass-blowers twisted their wares into fantastic shapes for the dark subterranean bars and the brilliantly lit houses of fantasy. The sound of a parrot or of a Spanish guitar carried the drinkers away into strange, far-off places. Social needs were met, but the standard of the brew was well below the one produced by the same machines in Italy. Even with an Italian behind the machine, the coffee served was invariably poor.

As coffee declined in England in the eighteenth century, it found new favour in Germany, where for many years it had been an indication of high social status. The new favour came from within the enlightened middle classes and the impetus for the spread of the drink came especially from women. The new burgher class of women recently arrived from country to town, freed from work in the fields, found that the *Kaffeeklatsch* was the ideal place to enjoy their new found freedom and leisure. It is in this arena that they tentatively entered the world of ideas, and discussed Goethe and Beethoven as well as babies and scandal – talk which was termed 'coffee-gossip' by a society which felt threatened by, and perhaps a little jealous of the new feminine liberation.

So popular did the drink become that throughout the nineteenth century Germany was far ahead of the rest of Europe in coffee consumption. Coffee had replaced flour soup and beer for breakfast. It was sipped at meal times and at Sunday afternoon family outings in the spacious cafés that became a lively feature of every German city, as famous for their newspapers and magazines as for their delectable pastries.

Coffee had come to America with immigration since the early eighteenth century. The first coffee houses were modelled after the London ones, but were more like taverns and inns, serving liquor and meals as well as coffee, tea and chocolate, and even letting rooms. Less joyous and more puritan in character than their European prototypes, they were more devoted to work and business than to witty, idle talk. Like the London coffee houses they were an important part of the life of the country as gathering places for merchants and businessmen. The more important ones had special meeting rooms. These long rooms, a feature which distinguished coffee houses from taverns, were used for meetings of merchants, colonial magistrates and overseers, and all types of public and private business. Occasionally court trials or auctions were held here, and they were also places of Mercantile Insurance where records were held and ships bought and sold. The Chamber of Commerce held sessions in a New York upper long room.

Men carried on their business at the coffee house and went on to the tavern for fun. Eventually they became purely mercantile buildings, while their social and gastronomic functions were divided between clubs, restaurants and hotels.

At first only 'a drink for the well-to-do, except in sips', coffee languished for a time in America while tea rose in favour. It gained an immense impetus following King George's Stamp Act of 1765, the Tea

Tax of 1767 and the resulting boycott of tea which was responsible for making the Americans a nation of coffee drinkers.

It was at the Boston 'Tea Party' of 1773, when the citizens of Boston boarded the British ships waiting in the harbour and threw all the British East India tea cargoes overboard, that coffee was crowned once and for all 'King of the American breakfast table'. It was here, too, that coffee became forever linked for the Americans with the War of Independence, with liberty and democracy.

Spain was the last country in Europe to adopt coffee houses. The innovative drink had not only to compete with taverns that sold wine and brandy but with establishments selling *horchata*, a refreshing cold white drink made from crushed tiger nuts, and especially with those selling chocolate which the Spaniards had discovered in South America in the sixteenth century. It was only in the early nineteenth century that cafés opened selling the 'foreign drink' coffee, which became the drink of intellectuals and left-wing political dissidents (anarchists and socialist revolutionaries were famously associated with cafés). Chocolate shops remained the haunts of traditionalists and priests and the conservative right wing. In the last decades of the century cafés displaced the traditional chocolate shops and by the twentieth century Spanish cities like most cities right across Europe all had their coffee houses.

We are seeing a renaissance of the fashion of the coffee house all over the world. As an example of the trend, in Vienna (where many of the old coffee houses closed in the sixties and seventies because people were more attracted by inns and bars) coffee houses have been rediscovered by the young and many have reopened, often in the old spot. They are attracting young people again and have re-established their old role as meeting places.

## Poison or Elixir?

In an English newspaper advertisement of 1657, coffee was described as 'having many excellent vertues, closes the Orifice of the Stomack, fortifies the heart within, helpeth Dijestion, quickneth the Spirits, maketh the heart lightsome, is good against Eyesores, coughs or Colds, Rhumes, Consumptions, Head-ache, Dropsie, Gout, Scurvy, King's Evil and many others'. As for the way to use it, this electuary (medicine mixed with honey) was devised: 'Take equal quantity of Butter and Sallet-Oyl, melt them together but not boyle them; Then stirre them well that they may incorporate together: Then melt therewith three times as much Honey, and stirre it well together. Then add thereunto powder of Turkish cophie to make it a thick electuary.'

# *C*OFFEE

Coffee was regarded as a medicine from its very beginning. This prejudice, which must have killed the pleasures to be had, was often reversed, but for motives that were not always related to health. When a thesis was put forward by the physicians of Marseilles in 1679 that 'the vile and worthless foreign novelty . . . the fruit of a tree discovered by goats and camels . . . burned up the blood . . . induced palsies, impotence and leanness . . . hurtful to the greater part of the inhabitants of Marseilles', they were, it appears, influenced by the local wine merchants.

Variously described as an 'elixir of life' as well as a poison, controversy has always raged over its effects. Threats, however, usually seem to have fallen on deaf ears, a familiar response being Voltaire's: 'I have been poisoning myself for more than eighty years and I am not yet dead.' Even Bach wrote a 'Coffee Cantata' in 1732, mocking a physicians' campaign to discredit coffee in Germany.

Among various investigations carried out over the years to settle the controversy, a notable one was made in Sweden in the eighteenth century. Identical twin brothers were condemned to death for murder. King Gustav III commuted their sentences to life imprisonment on condition that one twin be given a large daily dose of tea and the other of coffee. The tea drinker died first at the age of eighty-three. The question was settled, and today the Swedish people are amongst the world leaders in coffee consumption.

Many quips and sallies written from when coffee was new in France by such men as Hugo, Flaubert, Baudelaire, Balzac and Zola, testify to its power to stimulate creative work without unpleasant side effects.

Prince Talleyrand (1754–1839) expressed a general feeling when he said about a cup of coffee that it 'detracts nothing from your intellect; on the contrary, your stomach is freed by it and no longer distresses your brain; it will not hamper your mind with troubles but give freedom to its working. Suave molecules of Mocha stir up your blood, without causing excessive heat; the organ of thought receives from it a feeling of sympathy; work becomes easier and you will sit down without distress to your principal repast which will restore your body and afford you a calm delicious night.'

Today the controversy about the effects of coffee on health is still not resolved. Studies so far have been contradictory and inconclusive. During the 1980s one scare story after another linked coffee drinking with cancer, infertility, defects of the foetus, heart and other diseases; but every study claiming a link has been followed by further studies contradicting the claim. A very recent Scottish Heart Health study on 10,000 men and women has given coffee the all clear on links with heart disease. The beneficial effect of coffee is that it aids digestion, acts as a diuretic and offers stimulation without subsequent depression. The stimulating constituent, caffeine, which is also present in tea, chocolate and cola drinks, is arguably the world's most popular drug. It acts on the nervous system and on muscles, increasing mental activity and heightening perception. It does have ill effects, but almost always when there is over-indulgence. These ill effects may include insomnia, palpitations, headache, stomach upset, twitchiness and irritation.

General opinion is that in moderation coffee is not harmful. People differ in their caffeine sensitivity and the limit of moderation is a matter of individual constitution. Research has failed to eliminate the element of individual and psychological idiosyncrasy. Some people are immune to six or more cups a day and can drink coffee late into the evening without losing sleep, while three cups can make others develop palpitations and stay awake at night. How much we can drink can only be determined from personal experience.

To most of us the boost in concentration, the counter to the post-lunch dip in alertness and the surge in energy when we are feeling tired are the main attractions of coffee. It is certainly to the much-maligned caffeine that the beverage owes its survival through generations of incompetent brewing that destroyed all of its enjoyment as a drink.

The health scare has not taken hold in Britain and Europe as much as it has in America, where it has produced a vast increase in the market for decaffeinated coffee. Consumers in America are now also worried about solvents in decaffeinated coffees, about chemical pesticides and fertilizers, chemicals used in bleached filter paper and also those chemicals used for flavouring.

# COFFEE

## Custom and Ritual

Few travellers to the Levant fail to notice the luxury of tranquil enjoyment possessed by those who sit in front of a tiny cup filled with syrupy, frothy, black coffee, epitome of a way of life which prizes 'kayf' (peace of mind) above all things. They may sit in the silent darkness of a cavern-like shop, a *narghileh* (water pipe) passing from one to the other, or in an open-air café spilling across the street, surrounded by the animated shouts of 'Shish! Bish!' of backgammon players and the clapping of their dice and counters. Sometimes two chairs alone, one acting as armrest, foot-stool and table, outside a barber's shop, invite them to the moment of bliss. Certainly the Arab dictum: 'As with art 'tis prepared, so one should drink it with art', is honoured in this part of the world where coffee was first made.

Perhaps it is the early religious use of coffee that has given it a ceremonial character in the world of Islam. The dervishes of old drank coffee to keep awake during the nights given to religious devotion. The drink was kept warm in a large red earthenware vessel, each dervish receiving some in turn from his superior, who dipped their small bowls into the jar. They sipped the coffee while they chanted 'Allah w' akbar!' (God is great). After the dervishes were served, the jar was passed round to the rest of the congregation. Never was a religious ceremony performed without coffee being drunk.

Today, centuries after it became secularized, coffee drinking is still in the Middle East an activity enmeshed in ritual, practised at all times throughout the day.

In Arabia a watered down form of an early coffee-drinking ceremony still exists, starting with a string of gestures, greetings, praises to God, enquiries into health, traditional formulas of courtesy of an infinite and elegant variety. Rules of etiquette are observed in serving, in some cases involving each process of making, each performed with intense seriousness and deliberate nicety. The tiny, half-egg-sized cups are refilled three or four times. To refuse is an unforgivable insult. In this proverbially hospitable area, coffee is the symbol of hospitality. It is considered an outrage not to offer a cup of coffee to anyone who enters your house and an almost equal outrage to refuse. Coffee is made individually as soon as a visitor arrives, always freshly brewed in the small, long-handled copper or brass pots called *kanaka* or *ibrik*, sometimes roasted and pounded just before brewing. Tiny cups are set out on inlaid brass trays, as well as several glasses of water, sometimes scented with rosewater, to be drunk before, not after, so as not to wash down the taste of coffee. A bowl of jam may be set with little spoons hung on the side for guests to relish a little at a time as they take their coffee. On special occasions a few small pastries are piled on an elegant little plate. It is essential that each cup of coffee must have its share of the foam, which is called *wesh* (face). To ensure this, coffee is poured with a slight quiver of the hand. An important person is served first, the oldest next, and women last. Among Bedouins, cups are served only half filled. A filled one would mean: 'Drink up and go!' – a bitter insult also shown in the adage: 'Fill the cup for your enemy'. Here ritual insists that the pourer should be served first to ensure that the pot is not a deadly one for the person of most importance who is served next. It is not unknown for people to have been dispatched to another world with poison slipped into a cup of coffee. At this stage comes a great deal of arguing with shouts of 'Abadan! Abadan!' as each guest refuses, wishing to honour his neighbour more.

Since sugar is boiled at the same time as the coffee, guests are always asked their preference – whether they would like it sweet (*helou* or *sukar ziada*), medium (*mazbout*) or unsweetened (*murra*) – and they are served accordingly. The sweetness of the drink is sometimes determined by the occasion. At a happy one, such as a wedding or a birthday, it is served sweet, while at a funeral it must be drunk without any sugar at all.

In Turkey at one time, a man promised when he married never to let his wife go without coffee, and it was considered a legitimate cause for divorce if he neglected to do so. So important is coffee in Oriental life that it is common for beggars to ask for money to buy it. It is inconceivable that they should go without. Business and bargaining are always done over a cup of coffee served before the argument starts. Whether in

a shop or a market stall it creates a bond and an obligation between buyer and seller. Some people drink up to twenty-five cups a day, but these are so small, sometimes thimble-sized, that they do not amount to too much.

The habit of the coffee house is one that has required a certain leisure. Ceremony, too, has been required in the coffee houses of the Levant, where customers often sip their water and some a *narghileh* (water pipe) while waiting – for the service takes time. Only men go to the resorts of the 'lower orders'. Some bring their own pipe and tobacco, and sometimes hashish. The coffee-shop owner keeps two or three *narghilehs* which are used for both tobacco and hashish. Customers have to wait their turn. Etiquette prevails. A newcomer salutes each person on entering a crowded coffee room and is saluted in return. In the past it was usual for the entire company to rise when an old man entered and to yield him the inside corner chair. Such courtesies take time, and one sometimes has to wait for the beans to be roasted and milled.

In early Arabia, Burckhardt relates that respectable people were never seen in a coffee shop, but they were always filled with the lower classes and seafarers. An Arab who could not afford to ask a friend to dine would invite him to the coffee shop when he saw him pass, and would be highly offended if the invitation was rejected. The waiter, in presenting the coffee to the guest would cry aloud for all to hear: 'Jabba!' (gratis).

These ways have been spread by the Ottomans throughout their old Empire around the Mediterranean shores. Today in Cyprus a man sitting in a coffee shop will call to passers-by 'Kopiaste', inviting them to join him. If you happen to be in a strange village and sit in a coffee shop, you will probably find that your coffee has been paid for by someone else. As children, we were usually afraid of the scenes that occurred when the heads of families, enjoying a coffee and cake together, fought to pay everyone's bill. It is still the greatest honour to the host.

Very little of the oriental ceremony has been retained on our Western breakfast tables, but our casual entertaining is still over a cup of coffee and a degree of ritual is needed if it is to be properly made. The care we take in serving, be it in hand-warming bowls or elegant cups accompanied by coffee cakes, and the little rituals and courtesies of coffee time may not change its virtues, but they do add to its enjoyment.

# Two

# Cultivation

# Cultivation

## The Coffee Tree

One of the peculiarities of the coffee tree is that the fruit ripens several times a year. Another is that it bears at the same time both blossom and berries (also called cherries) at various stages of maturity. The entire style of the coffee trade is governed by this caprice of nature. If the cherries are allowed to grow overripe, the beans inside are spoilt. If they are unripe, the beans will not ripen once picked. So pickers of quality coffees must return to the same tree time and time again to pick only the

ripe cherries – an inordinate amount of labour for the 2 lb of clear green beans which is an average yearly yield for one tree. Bear it in mind when you next buy coffee.

There are more economical labour-saving methods of harvesting favoured by the growers of cheaper coffees, but they result in inferior, harsher tasting grades, burdened by impurities. In many parts of Africa, trees are shaken and berries picked from the ground before they are injured or rotten. In the greater part of Brazil, where the lower priced coffees are produced, branches are stripped of everything at once, leaves, flowers, overripe and underripe cherries. The mutilated trees take two years to recover from this savage treatment. A coffee tree is a rare, magnificent sight when it breaks out into a fragile and delicate white blossom, its fragrance as intoxicating as that of the orange and the jasmine which it resembles. It may bloom alone like a young bride or with the whole farm, a swaying sea of white petals, as beautiful as they are ephemeral. For in two or three days they will have fluttered off the bough, leaving their perfume to linger only a while longer.

Soon, tiny clusters of cherries appear, green at first, then yellow, red and deep crimson. When they are almost black, they are ready to pick. In Jamaica, bats are the first to know when the fruit is ripe. Their nightly sucking of the sweet pulp is a signal for the farmers to start harvesting. The oval berries sit in tight bunches hugging the branches from which the long, polished, dark green, lance-shaped leaves sprout in pairs. These are firm, but softer and paler on the underside and scalloped towards the edges. Branches also grow two by two on opposite sides of the trunk.

The evergreen trees are usually grown from seed in nursery beds, and transferred after a year to the plantation ground, in exactly the same way as the Arabs first raised and cultivated the plants. For the first four or five years of its life, the coffee tree is too busy growing roots and building a strong straight trunk and an umbrella of branches to bear a crop of beans. It will usually only produce a full crop in its sixth year and continue until the fifteenth year, when the yield declines. Left to nature it would grow to a height of fourteen to twenty feet and some even to forty feet. Apart from the regions where they are allowed to grow wild, they are generally kept pruned to a height of six feet to make picking easier and to reserve their strength for producing beans.

There are three main species of coffee plants grown commercially, each with its own varieties. *Coffea arabica* is the most important and produces the best quality beans. Found growing wild in Ethiopia, it is also the most widely cultivated. *Liberica* is a native of Liberia, while *robusta* originates in the Congo. As the latter name implies, they are stronger, withstand wider extremes of climate and are less susceptible to disease. They need less care in hoeing, weeding and pruning, and are often allowed to grow wild in forest conditions. Although 'hard' in flavour and of inferior quality to *arabica*, *robusta* has been adopted by the African continent in a big way. Its high yield makes it ideal for instant coffees. While *arabica* flourishes best at high altitudes from 2,000 to 6,500 feet above sea level – the higher the altitude the finer the quality – *liberica* and *robusta* do better below 2,000 feet.

Coffee trees only grow in tropical and sub-tropical lands. Within the limits of the 'coffee belt' they are able to grow in widely different climates, in different soils,

43

# COFFEE

at different altitudes and with varying amounts of rainfall. They thrive equally in the hot, humid valleys and rainy forests of Africa, in the cold, windy and foggy highlands of Central America, as well as in the changing weather of drought, torrential rain and stormy winds in the Caribbean. Here lies the reason for the different characteristics of the infinite variety of beans.

Ideal conditions are a temperature ranging between 65°F and 75°F, a good altitude and enough rain (from 40 to 120 inches a year). The time of rainfall is important. Alternating heavy rain and strong sun are needed for maturation, and a dry spell is needed for harvesting. Almost any type of soil will do, but the best is a mixture of disintegrated volcanic rock with an addition of decomposed mould and porous, permeable soil.

Sunshine is needed only a few hours a day. Hilly ground is ideal because it provides for only a short exposure, as well as making for good drainage. Coffee trees do not like their feet wet. Tall leafy trees are planted among the coffee trees as windbreaks and to give shade.

As for the hazards, frost and leaf disease are the usual killers.

## Preparing the Beans

Inside the sweet, gummy pulp of the fruit lie the precious green coffee beans. Flat-faced, marked by a thin incision, they hug each other face to face, protected by a tough outer hull, the parchment, and an interior, delicate, semi-transparent covering, the 'silver skin'.

Preparation for market is by removing all these outer layers, and is done by either of two methods. The 'wet' one, for washed coffees, is considered the better and is used for the hand-picked quality growths. The berries acquire a distinctive and attractive taste during thirty hours of steeping in fermentation tanks. The 'dry' method, which gives 'naturals', is more economical and used where water is scarce. Beans are spread out to dry in the sun for three weeks and turned over frequently. Cleaning is not as effective as in the 'wet' method but 'naturals' have the advantage of ageing better.

Beans are then sized, sorted, picked over to remove bad ones and graded, all by hand, with extra care taken for the higher grades. There is probably nothing we use that demands so much in terms of human effort. If value is related to the amount of handling and labour, coffee should indeed be placed high in our esteem.

# Coffee Classification – Market Terms

There are many complex factors involved in the production of coffee, from the wide variety of conditions – the mountains and the valleys, the jungles and plantations and different soils – to the different species and varieties of plants. These, combined with national styles of harvesting, processing, marketing and transportation, have resulted in a great tangle of nomenclature. There are over forty exporting countries, all of which use different systems of classification for more than a hundred types of coffee. The following are the basics.

### COFFEES ARE DIVIDED INTO THREE GENERAL GROUPS:

**Brazils** include all coffees grown in Brazil – nearly all of which are *arabicas*. Apart from the quality coffee Santos, they are the cheaper 'price' coffees which are used for high roasts and which make up the bulk of mass-produced commercial blends and instant coffees.

**Milds** include all the *arabica* species of coffees grown elsewhere. Among them are the premium *grands crus* or quality growths. They are not necessarily mild to taste, and some are bitter or acidy. Among these are the coffees with which the speciality market deals.

**Robustas** are mainly grown in Africa from a different species of plant with the same name. They are of inferior quality and have a higher caffeine content than Milds. They are used for mass-produced brands and instant coffees. Their high yield makes them formidable competitors on the price coffee market.

### COFFEES ARE FURTHER CLASSIFIED BY:

**Market names:** Usually these are of the port of embarkation, of the area of production or of plantations.

**Species of plant:** *Arabica* being the quality growths.

**Varieties of plant:** There are many, such as Bourbon, Maragogype, Excelsa, Nuevo Mondo.

**Altitude:** The high grown always being the finest.

**Methods of processing:** The 'washed' method is that generally used for the choice quality beans.

**Number of imperfections**: Such as blackened, broken and immature beans, sticks, stones and pods.

**According to size, shape and colour of beans**: Whether large or flat and through all the shades of light green, grey and bluish green. 'Hard-bean' indicates coffees of excellent body and acidity.

**By the crop**: Whether old or new and the age of the trees.

**By the age of the beans**: Most coffees improve with ageing between three and ten years. But few are aged these days. Old Java especially matures exquisitely. Others such as Boubon Santos weaken to a fragile insipidity.

**By their drinking qualities**: Whether they are heavy-bodied, acidy, bitter or sweet and fragrant.

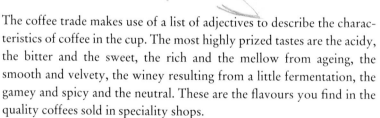

The coffee trade makes use of a list of adjectives to describe the characteristics of coffee in the cup. The most highly prized tastes are the acidy, the bitter and the sweet, the rich and the mellow from ageing, the smooth and velvety, the winey resulting from a little fermentation, the gamey and spicy and the neutral. These are the flavours you find in the quality coffees sold in speciality shops.

The less desirable tastes are described as flat, wild, grassy and muddy, harsh and fermented, sour, hidey or Rioy (from the harsher tastes of Rio). They are associated with imperfect methods of harvesting, processing and storing and find anonymity in instant coffees and branded blends or in high roasts where they lose some of their harshness. The pronounced Rioy taste does, however, have a following with people who are accustomed to the coarse harsh taste resulting from cherries both ripe and unripe being torn off the tree together, then picked from the ground and dried in the sun.

# Three

# Selecting
# and Buying

# Buying Coffee

For those within reach of a specialist coffee shop the best way to buy coffee is in the bean and freshly roasted. And the best thing to invest in is a home grinder. Although in its green state coffee ages well and is only adversely affected by dampness and strong odours, which it absorbs, once roasted it begins to lose its aroma – the volatile complex caffeol – and will have lost most of it within two weeks. When it is ground it loses the aroma even faster. So only buy a little at a time and grind it at home as you need it, or buy it already ground in smaller quantities and store it in an airtight jar. Some people recommend storing ground coffee in the refrigerator. I have found this not a good idea as condensation forms

and dampens the grounds which go stale more quickly. A good alternative is to freeze roasted beans in an airtight bag as soon as you get home (they keep well for 3 months) and to grind them frozen as you need them. A greater intensity of flavour and aroma is preserved.

A less exalted way of buying coffee is in commercial branded tins or foil-lined packets or plastic bags, vacuum-packed to seal in the aroma and exclude the oxygen which causes coffee to turn rancid and deteriorate. There is now an enormous variety of branded commercial blends to be found in supermarkets and elsewhere. They are cheap and readily accessible and you can buy them in advance and keep stocks, but quality and variety are sacrificed. To reach the widest market at a competitive price they must use more of the cheaper, less interesting, flavourless coffees. Though many are mediocre and some are really bad, you can get some very good mass-produced coffees these days. The best strive to maintain a standard of quality and consistency with a mix of as many as seven or eight coffees and an eye on the new quality-conscious market.

The speciality trade is something else. When I enter a coffee shop, especially when they roast on the premises, I get a great feeling of joy and excitement. As well as the exhilarating aromas (like incense in a church) the dramatic effect of sacks of pale green beans, of shiny brown beans pouring out of glittering containers, and the appealing coffee-making equipment, it is a special pleasure and privilege to be able to choose from a selection of quality beans and types of roast.

A good specialist shop should sell only the best grades of high-grown *arabica* beans. It is important with coffee (more so perhaps than with any other food product) that you can trust your merchant to sell you good-quality beans, because you have no way of making sure except by tasting – certainly not from the labelling. Be choosy about who you buy from. Choose a shop by its ability to select good coffees, to roast them well and to sell them freshly roasted. It is not easy to be a coffee vendor. They must be permanently on their toes because the coffee market is ever-changing and unreliable. Coffee is a product of nature, slave to its vagaries, and there is an element of mystery in each crop and each shipment, even from the same farm. No two beans are the same, even if they are picked from the same branch. Coffee is affected not only by climate, soil and cultivation, but also by methods of picking and processing, storage and transportation. The standard of some coffees deteriorates

when a fall in price makes them unprofitable to the producer, who then neglects good marketing procedures and proper grading. Some coffees become scarce and too expensive because they have become fashionable, because frost has killed the trees, because there is civil war and drought in the country of origin, or because it is far more profitable to grow drugs like qat (in Yemen) and coca for cocaine (in Colombia and Peru). There are also some instances of moving coffees to plantations with famous names and of smuggling them across borders to a neighbouring country with a prestigious reputation and not enough coffee to satisfy demand. There being no regularity and stability in the quality and availability of growths, you can only hope that your coffee vendor keeps his standards of quality. He may sometimes have to upgrade his usual purchase or find a cheaper equivalent to one that has priced itself out of the market, or a replacement for one that has become scarce. This helps to explain why a coffee in one shop is different from a same origin coffee in another, and why a prestigious coffee may not live up to its promise.

# Choosing Coffee

A Spanish proverb '*Sobre los gusto no hay disputa*' rules that there is no argument in the matter of taste. The best coffee is the one you like best, and that is something you can only discover for yourself. I cannot find the right words nor give an identity to the sensations different coffees have given me; but there have been many and they have stirred many memories. I would far rather put a steaming cup in your hand and say, 'Smell it! Taste it! Look at it!' Even Brillat-Savarin confessed he could no more describe fragrance 'than the perfume of yesterday's violets'.

The prestigious quality coffees have a distinctive richness and complexity which encompasses a whole gamut of flavours and fragrances. These depend to a certain extent on roasting and brewing, but most of all it is the type of bean and its origin that counts. There is a trend now to describe coffees in the language of wine in terms such as tart, tangy, flowery, fruity or spicy, winey and gamey, nutty, chocolatey, musty and mellow, but the trade focuses on only four main desirable classes of taste; it is the way these come into play in varying degrees that distinguishes the different coffees.

**THIS IS WHAT TO LOOK FOR WHEN YOU TASTE:**

**Sweetness** is due to the sugar content which caramelizes on roasting.

**Acidity** is derived from a complex of compounds misnamed 'caffetanic acid'. Coffee low in acidity tastes smooth, soft and mellow but some acidity is desirable as it adds sharpness and life. Coffee tastes flat without acidity.

**Bitterness** is present naturally in some beans. It is also due to decomposition products formed during roasting. These types of bitterness are considered appealing and have their following. But the bitterness that is the result of chlorogenic acid and the soluble mineral content of the bean when there is over-extraction in the brewing process is unpleasant.

**A neutral taste** is prized particularly for its blending qualities and capacity to marry well with other tastes.

**Aroma** or fragrance is the gases, products of aromatic oils, released by roasting. The best coffees have two or three times more aromatic oils than others. Some aromas are delicate and fleeting, some are complex and powerful. They are experienced as part of taste.

**Body** is a quality characterized by a thick, heavy feel and lingering rather than evanescent taste.

Choosing coffee may seem perplexing and daunting at first. Some merchants offer a few well-selected types of beans, others a huge range. Most produce a brochure which lists their coffees with characteristics and different roasts as well as recommendations as to whether a type is especially good for black coffee or with milk, for breakfast or after dinner, with espresso or other methods of brewing. Sometimes countries of origin and plantation names as well as details about altitude, soil and production methods are also given. But no amount of information can replace tasting. There is an important element of culture and acquired taste in the enjoyment of coffee. If you don't have a strong tradition of coffee drinking behind you, you will be more open to broadening your experience and exploring the wondrous world of coffee. The pleasures of a perfect cup may be fleeting moments, but they can be repeated and they are worth pursuing.

$\mathscr{C}$OFFEE

# An A to Z Guide
# to the Choice Quality Beans

Here is a list, by country of origin, of the quality coffees of the world, from Africa, India and the Americas as well as the islands that lie within the tropics. They are all Milds, apart from Santos which is the 'quality' Brazil. All are of the *arabica* variety. There are some broad regional similarities but each has distinctive characteristics.

With the greater government control of more recent years and with associations and co-operatives forming, some of the famous historic names of coffee plantations have been absorbed into the different countries' productions.

## BRAZIL

A Portuguese Captain-Lieutenant of the Coastguard, Francisco de Malo Palheta, paying a visit to the Governor of Cayenne, French Guiana, in 1727, was so pleased with the coffee served to him that by ingratiating himself with the governor's lady, he managed to obtain secretly seeds of the coffee plant. With these he returned to the Portuguese Colony of Para on the Amazon river. Today, many types and grades make up 30 per cent of the world's total consumption.

Santos, especially Bourbon Santos (named after the French island colony of Bourbon, now Réunion, where the seed was grown), are the most popular for their sweet, clear, neutral flavour. They can be drunk straight but are also excellent partnered with any Mild. The true Bourbon is obtained from only the first few crops, which are grown from Mocha seed. After the third and fourth year, the bean changes in character. By the sixth it has become a Flat Bean Santos. Red Santos is sweet, Bourbon Santos is bitter, New Crop Santos is acidy. Ageing decreases the acidity.

The rest (Rio, Parana, Victoria, Bahia) are the less labour-intensive, mass-produced 'price' coffees; heavy, pungent and harsh, muddy and often peculiarly smoky from being dried on wood fires. They do, however, age well, losing their grassy flavour. Occasionally, accidents of nature such as the development of certain bacteria result in a special quality.

Although coffee will grow almost everywhere in Brazil, it suffers more than in any other country from unseasonable rains and storms, and winter winds from the Andes. It is also permanently endangered by crippling frosts which dramatically lose a great deal of its production at least once every five years – on occasion as much as 80 per cent.

The chief plantations are on plateaux 1,800 feet to 4,000 feet above sea level. The two most fertile soils are 'terra roxa', a top soil of red clay three feet thick with gravelly subsoil in Sao Paolo and 'Massape', a yellowish soil.

Apart from the better grades, coffee is essentially a 'quantity' and not a 'quality' product. The planter's eye is on economy. In the giant *Fazendas*, care is not exercised in either cultivation or harvesting. Trees are not shaded, so the yield is greater, but the ripening is even more uneven. For quick picking whole branches are ripped off with unripe and over-matured beans, and to these are added those already fermented that have fallen on the ground.

## BURUNDI

The high grades are rich and aromatic with a good body and high acidity. There is also a soft mild, less acid variety. Cultivation was introduced by Belgian colonists in 1930. Production had dropped but has recently been revived.

## COLOMBIA

Colombia is the world's second largest producer after Brazil, famous for consistently good fine mild coffees – good enough to drink straight – whose distinctive characteristic is a caramel sweetness, rich flavour, slight acidity and heavy body. They produce a quarter more liquor of given strength than Brazilian Santos.

There are many grades ranging from poor to first class. The finest are grown in the foothills of the Andes, 3,500 to 4,500 feet above sea level, in the shade of banana and rubber trees. Some of the best coffee lands consist of rich loamy soil mixed with disintegrated volcanic rock or porous subsoils. Hundreds of thousands of small farms are family enterprises, organized into a federation on a co-operative basis. Great care is taken in cultivation, picking and processing by the wet method.

The most exported grades are Supremo and Excelso. The finest is the larger-bean Supremo, prized for its sweet, delicate and aromatic taste, slightly nutty bitterness and light body. Excelso, soft and slightly acid, is not always consistent. Other famous names are Medellin, Armenia and Manizales, Bogota and Bucaramanga. The government makes every effort to encourage the coffee trade to maintain its high standards and position in the world market, to keep up the living standards of coffee-growers and help the fight against the narcotics trade.

## COSTA RICA

The high altitude Costa Ricans are among the world's finest classic coffees: rich in body, of fine mild flavour, sharply acid and fragrant. The acidity level increases with the altitude. The lower regions produce coffee of more neutral tastes. The most famous zone is the Central Plateau around San José, where the soil is a rich black loam made up of continuous layers of volcanic ashes and dust three to fifteen feet deep. Beans are especially known for their fine preparation and screening. Large plants (*beneficios*) process the coffee produced by small farms. *Fincas* are farms big enough to have their own processing plants. Famous names of top '*grands crus*' are Tarrazu, Tres Rios, Santa Rosa, Montbello and Juan Vinas.

The first plants were brought from Cuba in 1779 by a Spanish traveller, Navarro. Later, growths from Jamaica came with a Spanish missionary, Padre Carazo.

## CUBA

A pleasant coffee – like the Jamaican in character but not as acid because the mountains are not very high. It is sold largely to Russia, eastern Europe and France, where it is appreciated because its character resembles that of the historic but now non-existent coffees of the French overseas departments in the Caribbean (Martinique, Guadeloupe, Réunion).

In 1792 Haitian slaves rebelled against their French colonists and took refuge in Cuba. It was these refugees who first developed coffee plantations there.

## DOMINICAN REPUBLIC

The best grades are strong and heavy bodied. Barahona, which is acidy and resembles Jamaican high mountain, is the most attractive and has the best reputation. Bani and Ocoa are soft and mellow.

## EL SALVADOR

Their best coffees, labelled 'Strictly High Grown' are classic Central American coffees – pleasant with medium acidity, full body, mild sweet taste and delicate fragrance. They are much appreciated in France.

## ETHIOPIA

Ethiopian coffees are among the most distinctive in the world. They can be quite splendid – winey, fruity, acidy with a singular 'wild' exotic taste – but the quality is inconsistent. The reason they do not always live up to their promise is because lower grades are sometimes sent instead of the top ones.

The indigenous wild trees of Ethiopia are the progenitors of all the *arabicas* grown in the world. Much of the coffee produced is still gathered from wild trees and most is processed in primitive ways (a wooden pestle and mortar is still used). Before civil war, drought and famine crippled the industry, coffee production had been expanding and attention had been given to improved methods of harvesting.

A variety of coffees are produced, each with its own characteristics. Harrar, graded as 'Longberry' and 'Shortberry', is the most famous. It resembles the Yemen Moka which it often replaced in the days when it was more readily available. That is why it is sometimes called Harrar or Ethiopian Moka. It is processed by the traditional dry method and varies from extremely rough to soft, mild and fragrant with highly acid, winey, fruity, gamey, and spicy qualities.

Djimah and Lekempti coffees are thick-bodied and highly acidic with earthy wild gamey flavours. They are produced in areas where wild trees are barely touched and berries are just picked off the ground.

The 'washed' coffees are remarkable for their soft, fragrant, rich, not too acid, balanced qualities. Of these the Gimbi have winey tones; Sidamo is fruity; Yirgacheffe is fragrant and flowery and highly appreciated in the USA where Ethiopians are seen as mysterious and exotic. Ethiopians generally, like Yemen Moka, are the traditional and favoured coffees of the Middle East.

Some people believe that coffee derives its name from the region of Kaffa of which it is native. All the early legends about the discovery of the drink are based in Ethiopia. Though not much esteemed as a drink at first, it was consumed as a food. The beans were roasted, pulverized and mixed with butter to form hard balls to be eaten by the wandering Gallas on their journeys. Coffee was, however, an important export sent via Mocha – hence the early misconception of its origin.

## GUATEMALA

The high grown 'Strictly Hard Bean' grades are among the finest coffees in the world – complete, perfectly balanced, full bodied, very acidy with a soft mild flavour and delightful bouquet. The most famous are the Cobans, Antiguas, Atilans and Huehuetenango. In severe weather, rubbish and pitch are burnt near the plantations. The dense smoke saves the trees from frost and gives the coffee a smokey flavour. Cultivation was developed by German emigrants in the nineteenth century.

## HAITI

The best high grown grades are remarkable. Sweet, mellow, rich in flavour, fairly acid and heavy bodied, they resemble the famous Blue Mountain which they are sometimes used to extend. The more carelessly cultivated grades of not too high quality are used for high roasts in

Europe and especially in France where they are much appreciated for their sweet caramel taste.

Cultivation was started in 1715 by Jesuits. The deep volcanic soil and wet climate are very favourable. Trees have always been allowed to grow wild. The political situation and the general lack of enterprise have resulted in low production.

## HAWAII

Kona is the very special coffee grown on the dark volcanic lava in the Kona district of Hawaii which nestles between the twin towering volcanoes Mauna Loa and Mauna Kea. It is a deliciously rich, medium-bodied and slightly acidy coffee with a heady aroma and complex winey, spicy taste. It should be savoured pure and straight. The beans are beautiful and lustrous. It seemed not long ago that coffee might be a vanishing industry in Hawaii, but in response to the demand for quality coffees in America and Kona's new found phenomenal prestige, production revived and prices shot up. Kona is now more expensive than it is worth.

## INDIA

Mysore is the most celebrated of Indian coffees, so much so that other regional coffees are sold under the name of Mysore. In 1610 a Muslim pilgrim Baba Budan brought back Yemeni beans from his pilgrimage to Mecca and planted them near his hut in the state of Mysore (now Karnataka). The first systematic plantation was established in 1820 by the English in southern India. Other names are Coorg, Bababudan, Shevaroys and Billigris. As coffee is generally sold through central auctions where lots are made up from different provenances these names are often lumped together.

In the days when coffee was transported by sailing ship, it took six months for cargoes from India to reach Europe. During that time beans turned yellow and acquired a mellow taste. That special taste was so appreciated that India continues to reproduce the flavour and golden colour in a treatment called 'monsooning' by which unwashed beans are first exposed to dampness in warehouses then to the hot air of the monsoon winds which is allowed to circulate around loosely stacked sacks of beans for a month. Monsooned Malabar is one of the best: heavy-bodied with a deep colour, rich spicy flavour and aroma and a little acidity.

## INDONESIA

Plantations were introduced by the Dutch in 1699 with plants from the Malabar coast of India. The once very important trade diminished when Brazil and Central America became dominant in the market. Indonesian coffees enjoy great historic prestige but their quality is not consistent.

**Java** produces a spicy strong-flavoured, full-bodied coffee with a well-balanced acidity. In the years before 1915, when slow-moving sailing ships transported coffee to New York, the sweating of the beans during the long voyage resulted in a much-prized unique musty flavour. Today the rare Old Java, aged for about three years (it was once a minimum of ten), reproduces some of the characteristics of the sailing ship coffees with a mature, weet, mellow flavour and spicy fragrance, good body and strength.

**Sumatra** coffees are unusually strong, complex and heavy bodied with a unique musty flavour. They are among the most famous in the world but they are an acquired taste. They are best drunk black after dinner. Mandheling and Ankola are the finest with an almost syrupy richness, exquisite flavour and aroma.

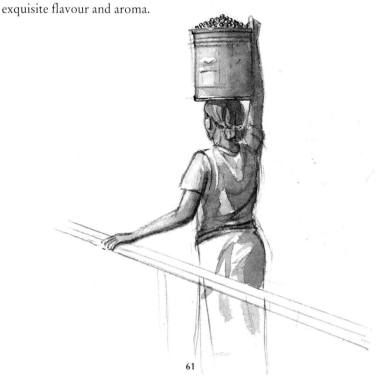

**Celebes** Toraja is like Sumatra but lighter and more acid.

## JAMAICA

During the French revolution Frenchmen fleeing from Haiti found refuge in Jamaica. They started the plantations; later, cultivation was encouraged and fostered by the British. In 1969 the Japanese were granted favourable loans to develop production and they guaranteed a market. Since then nearly all the production of the legendary Blue Mountain has gone to Japan and scarcity, myth and snob appeal have kept prices sky high.

Blue Mountain coffee – so called because it is blue-green and grown at high altitudes – is easy to like, very simple with no complex flavours, good acidity and distinctly sweet and aromatic. But you hardly ever get it at its best and you hardly ever get the genuine article. It is magic and romance that you pay for. High Mountain supreme has similar but less pronounced attributes. The low grown 'naturals' are popular for French roasts. They remind the French of the vanished historic coffees in their overseas territories of Martinique, Réunion and Guadeloupe, which were once among the best growths in the world.

## KENYA

Kenya is a most delightful coffee, extremely popular in Britain for its sharp acidity, excellent flavour and fragrance.

Coffee came to Kenya not through neighbouring Ethiopia but from the island of Réunion with Roman Catholic missionaries as late as 1893. Now the industry is one of the most sophisticated in the world and standards of quality are consistently high. (Only ripe cherries are picked, grading is strict.)

In the much prized Kenya Peaberry, one of the ovules never develops. The single ovule, because it has no pressure on one side, is round and absorbs all the goodness of the cherry, which accounts for its intense flavour and special liquoring. It is also called Chagga after the tribe that grows it.

## MALAWI

This coffee is similar to Kenya but lighter and less fine.

## MEXICO

Lately private exporters have been concentrating on high quality. The finest now compare with the best of Central America, with fine acidity, sweet, mellow flavour and pleasing bouquet. Coatepec, Huatusco and Orizaba, Oaxaca and Chiapas are the best known. Their Margogype is the best of that special variety of *arabica* found in Central America but the quality varies according to the plantation.

## NICARAGUA

Their neutral taste makes them ideal blenders. The high grown have a good body and acidity with a mild flavour. The Jinotegas and Matagalpas could be among the best Central Americans but the quality is irregular.

## PANAMA

Their fine quality with good acidity, full body and mild pleasant flavour can rival Costa Rica.

## PAPUA NEW GUINEA

This country is a recent producer. Coffee was first cultivated commercially in the 1950s and it is growing fast in popularity and stature. The high grown milds, grown from Kenya seeds by smallholders, resemble Kenya coffees but with less acidity and more sweetness. They are full-bodied and aromatic with a smooth mild flavour. Special names are Sigri, Kiap and Arona.

## PERU

The Chanchamayos can be as good as the best classic Central Americans – full-bodied, delicate and gently acid – but large exporters have mixed mediocre coffees with good ones which has damaged their prestige. Buyers must go directly to the producers.

Production remains low and quality irregular because of the terror wrought by revolutionary groups and because plantations have turned over to coca for cocaine.

## TANZANIA

A fine coffee similar to Kenya – rich in flavour and aromatic but producing a thinner liquor and not as acid. Most exquisite is Kibo Chagga,

OFFEE

cultivated by the Chagga tribe in forest clearings on the cool and misty upper slopes of Mount Kilimanjaro.

## UGANDA

High grown Bugisu is the only quality coffee produced in Uganda (the rest is *robusta*) near the Kenya border. It is full-bodied and acid, like Kenya. Some of it is smuggled over the border and sold as Kenya.

## VENEZUELA

Venezuelan coffee is very complete and original and different from other American coffees – mild and mellow, slightly acid, sweet and delicate with an enticing aroma. Much prized are Meridas, the best of the Maracaibos, which have a peculiar delicate flavour. Caracas has a light body and distinctive, attractive flavour and is especially popular in France and Spain.

Production went right down after the seventies when the oil boom made coffee irrelevant to the Venezuelan economy but it is now being revived. Quality varies greatly depending on the plantations.

## YEMEN

Yemen coffee is called Mocha, named after the Yemen city of Muka from which it was first exported, and which supplied all of the world's coffee trade until the close of the seventeenth century.

The dry Arabian soil and the lack of moisture in the air produce a bean which is extra-hard and small. Mocha has been recognized since the beginning of coffee drinking as the best available, with a clear, distinctive, winey, deliciously piquant, gamey flavour, a unique acid character that some consider aggressive, and a very heavy body. It is valued as after dinner coffee, for a time of day when delicate flavours would go unnoticed. It blends well with most Milds, especially with Mysore and Indonesian growths (Java and Sumatra), and is a favourite for Turkish coffee blends often partnered with Mysore.

The crude and primitive cultivation has seen little improvement over the centuries. Trees are mostly grown in small gardens carved into the steep hillside of almost inaccessible mountain regions. An ingenious system of irrigation fed by mountain springs carries water to trees terraced with soil and small walls. All the work is done by hand. Beans are dried in the sun on housetops or on beaten earth.

Curiously, the drink is little appreciated in the area where coffee was first cultivated. A weak decoction is generally made of the hulls. Small farmers are sadly neglecting coffee trees in favour of the drug 'qat' which is much in vogue for chewing. Production has also remained restricted because of political disturbances and uneconomical cultivation.

### ZAIRE

Some good coffees are grown in the districts of Kivu and Ituri with a high acidity and pleasant flavour. They can be used to add sharpness to a neutral blend.

### ZIMBABWE

Pleasantly acid, it is similar to Kenya but not as richly flavoured or full-bodied.

Many other quality coffees exist whose production is so small that it is unlikely that you would find them. Puerto Rico, which had abandoned the trade, has revived cultivation and is returning to the export market with a very limited amount of expensive strictly gourmet coffee. Mauritius has only one commercial plantation which produces excellent coffee. In his book *Les Cafés Produits dans le Monde*, Philippe Jobin mentions coffee from Saint Helena, the distant island in the Atlantic to which Napoleon I was deported and where he died. One plantation, Sandy Bay, under government control, produces one ton of beans a year of which an English Roaster, Taylor of Harrogate in Yorkshire, prides itself on being the sole buyer.

Some coffee-producing countries are missing in this list because their production has deteriorated over the years – Angola because of its continuing war, Cameroon because Africanization of plantations and lack of profitability with tumbling coffee prices has meant that the regular care needed to maintain the unique quality and flavour has not been kept up.

A few countries may find a place in the future list of quality coffees: South Africa, which was boycotted because of its apartheid policy, will now be able to export its excellent Kenya-style coffee; China, which introduced *arabica* in the 1950s and abandoned it during the Cultural Revolution, began to develop it again in the 1980s; Vietnam has started to cultivate fine varieties of *arabicas*.

A note for travellers looking for the perfect cup: you are not likely to find good coffee in the countries of origin because all too often exporting countries keep the lowest rejects for local consumption. Conversely, in Australia coffee produced for local consumption only is delightful, uniting strength, flavour and aroma.

# Blending

Many of the coffees I have listed are 'self-drinkers' which are so good they can be drunk straight and pure and enjoyed for their distinctive qualities; but even these single highly-prized growths can benefit from marriage with one or more other types. Each type of coffee has its special attributes and weaknesses and a blend is meant to result in a balanced composition of the best qualities. The art of blending is to combine coffees with complementary characteristics – acid with sweet and neutral, light with heavy bodied, dark with light roasts – in such a way that all the better qualities of flavour, aroma, body and appearance produce a delightful complex drink.

Speciality shops and roasters usually have their own house blends which seek to create, by blending various coffees, a single mix with a combination of appealing traits at a reasonable price. Customers expect the blends to remain the same. It is a challenge for the blender to maintain consistency with the changing factors involving the beans and to find replacements for those that become unavailable or too expensive. Blends are usually a closely guarded secret. Some are named after the prestigious bean that gives the distinguishing flavour; some after the time of day at which they are best suited, such as 'Breakfast' and 'After Dinner'; others have labels suggestive of prestige, romance and exoticism. Some blends are labelled by the varieties included but most are kept secret. By not identifying the coffees they are using, blenders have greater latitude to select the best tasting beans available while keeping the price down. There are quite a few 'Blue Mountain Style' and 'Kona Style' blends; these approximate the qualities one used to find in those prestigious articles but at a lower price and containing no beans at all from Jamaica or Hawaii. Some blenders mix the green beans and roast them together but purists maintain that it is better to roast the different beans separately, giving each the time it requires. It is usual to roast the finer premium beans to a degree which brings out their best qualities and preserves all their flavours while cheaper beans, with less to lose, are high roasted to give a bitter kick to the blend. Big commercial roasters follow the same principles for their brand blends but these are dictated more by their concern for a wide mass market appeal and competitive prices. Many are filled with Brazils and *robustas*.

It is worth creating your own blends and experimenting to find one that you really like. Consult the A to Z Guide. Ask your dealer to help you. Talk to him about the qualities you like and dislike in his blends and ask his advice about variations on these until you achieve a perfect balance of flavour, body and aroma.

Following are the partnerships that tradition has cemented and from which you can derive inspiration.

Mocha and Mysore, the Turkish coffee favourites, are high roasted and pulverized.

Honoré de Balzac made famous a blend of Brazilian Bourbon, Martinique and Mocha which his servant purchased in three different shops. Martinique is no longer available but can be replaced by Haiti or Cuban.

A Neapolitan favourite is a mixture of Brazilian Santos and Ethiopian Harrar in a dark roast.

Other combinations that you might like to try are:
Java and Mocha
Brazilian Bourbon Santos and Colombian Bogota
Colombian Medellin and Ethiopian Mocha
Costa Rican, Java and Mocha
Sumatra and Mocha
Bogota Colombian, washed Venezuelan Maracaibo, Brazilian Santos
Coatepec Mexican, Cobans from Guatemala and Mandheling from
    Java

Kenya, Mocha and Guatemala
Costa Rica, Sumatra and Hawaii
Java and Kivu or Tanzanian

Colombian, Kenya and Costa Rica are particularly versatile blenders. The milder-tasting coffees from the Americas are good all-rounders with or without milk. The new crops are usually acid. The stronger ones like Mocha, Mysore, Java and Sumatra are best drunk black. Ethiopian Mocha may be used instead of Mocha. Indonesian coffees are sometimes bitter; so are old Bogotas and Brown Santos. Red Santos, Santo Domingo and Haiti are sweet.

A mixture of light and dark roasted coffee is very pleasant. Try three-quarters light and one-quarter dark, as the dark tends to dominate, unless you are blending for Turkish coffee or espresso, in which case it is nicer to have more of the darker one.

# Roasting

Ideally every household, restaurant and café should have its own roasting equipment since coffee is better made with freshly roasted beans. Green beans are roasted to develop aroma, flavour and body, a practice started in the thirteenth century. During the process, chemical changes take place: soluble oils are developed, caramel is formed, adding its distinctive taste and giving coffee its rich brown shades, and gases are liberated inside the bean. These are the components of caffeol, which gives the precious aroma.

In the seventeenth and eighteenth centuries in England, coffee was browned over charcoal fires, in ovens and on top of stoves, in earthenware tart dishes, old pudding pans and frying pans. In Germany, where Frederick the Great had banned the consumption of coffee by ordinary citizens, it was the aroma of home roasting that led his 'coffee smellers' to discover those who were breaking the law.

Today it is mainly the poor from the less developed countries who do their own roasting. Various devices exist for this. Old-style ones include

a small rotating perforated drum and a covered pan with a top handle which turns an oar pushing the beans over and around.

I have collected a few very primitive roasters including a Bedouin one which is like a giant spoon on three legs with a long metal stirrer attached by a chain.

There are now very good electric home roasting machines but anyone can attempt their own roasting at home in a heavy frying pan if they are prepared to learn the hard way, by practice. It is not easy to achieve an even roast, but when you do, you will be rewarded by a magnificent aroma and a fine cup of coffee.

Use an old heavy pan. Have an open window or use an extractor to carry away smoke and chaff. Use only one layer of green beans; otherwise they will not roast evenly.

The best results are obtained from a medium slow fire at the beginning, then a quick high heat for development at the end. The quicker the roast, the better the coffee. Shake the pan constantly, stir and turn over the beans with a spatula or a wooden spoon so that the heat reaches the beans evenly on all sides. With Peaberry beans, which are rounded and roll about nicely in the pan, it is easier to get a more uniform roast. Do not panic if the beans start to brown unevenly. Some always do to begin with. They will shrivel up, become a yellowish brown, then swell, darken, and occasionally 'pop' open. Test a bean for readiness by biting into it or cracking it between your fingers. It must be thoroughly roasted inside as well as outside. Watch the colour. The art is to stop just before the desired degree of roasting has been reached. It takes practice. It might be sensible to strive at first for a medium brown. Never let the beans darken more than chocolate brown and be careful that the coffee oils do not catch fire. Remove from the fire and cool quickly (on marble is a good way) to preserve the aroma by closing the pores of the beans. The brown nuggets, evenly coloured from inside to outside, are ready for grinding as soon as they have cooled.

Another way of roasting coffee is in the oven. Put the beans in a roasting tin in a very hot oven, 240°C, 475°F (gas 9) for twenty minutes, shaking them occasionally. This will be enough for a mild to medium roast. For a high roast, reduce to 200°C, 400°F (gas 6) and leave another twenty minutes.

You may like to throw in spices towards the end of roasting, as Ethiopians do. Use cloves (five to eight for eight cups of coffee), a small piece of cinnamon, ginger and nutmeg and sometimes cardamom or fennel seeds. Grind them together with the beans.

Most of us prefer to save ourselves the trouble and the disappointment of unevenly roasted beans, and rely on the skilled roaster at the specialist coffee shop. He watches over his beans being tossed about in the revolving cylinder placed alluringly at the shop window. He varies the heat slightly according to whether the coffee is new or old and dry, and thrusts in his 'trier', shaped like a long spoon, to see if they are done.

Computer generated and automatic coffee plant operations work on the same principles as the small-capacity machines. Here cold water is often used to 'head' the roast. It turns to steam and is not absorbed, but just slightly swells and brightens the beans. Some commercial roasters use a hot air system. These kinds of roasters give consistency of roast, but quality is sacrificed to a certain extent because nothing can replace smelling and looking.

Finishing or glazing is practised to a small extent in the trade. A method of moist friction polish is common, as well as coatings of sugar and egg to make coffee more attractive. In the French (or Belgian) sugar roast, sugar caramelizes with the heat and makes a shiny black bean. It is also supposed to preserve the roasted bean and retain the aroma and oils. In 'Italian roast' a little butter is sometimes added with sugar to the cylinder.

Although terms and degrees of roasting are interpreted differently by individual roasters, and while most use only two types of roast – **medium** and **dark** – four types are generally recognized:

**Light or Pale Roast** – also called Cinnamon and Half City
**Medium Roast** –also called Full City, American and Regular
**Dark or Full Roast** – also called High, Viennese, French and Continental
**Darkest Roast** – also called Italian and Espresso

Light and medium roasts, which preserve the acidity and allow the beans to keep their delicate flavours and aromas, are recommended for delicately flavoured coffees. They are especially suitable for breakfast and with milk. The darker roasts, where much of the acidity disappears and a strong bitter kick and sweet caramelized taste replace it, are best drunk black. They are recommended for after dinner. A dark full roast has a rich tangy flavour and a good balance between sweetness and sharpness. All the acidic qualities and distinctive coffee flavours have gone from the almost black, oily beans of the darkest espresso or Italian roast, but fans appreciate their pungent bitter flavour.

Southern Europe and the Levant, as well as the producing countries, favour dark roasts. Southern Italians roast to the point of carbonization while Northern Italians prefer a medium roast for their espressos. Anglo Saxons have traditionally always drunk light and medium roasts but now dark roasts, associated with educated European tastes, are fashionable and many espresso coffee lovers have become addicted to the bitter oily black beans that taste burnt. In America trendy roasters prefer dark roasts and it is they who set the trends. There are hot debates on the merits of the various degrees of roasting but the general view in the specialist trade is to use medium roasts when dealing with the finest coffees and darker roasts with cheaper coffees because much of the original flavour is driven off. Good roasting is about developing each type of coffee to its maximum potential – about preserving and bringing to their peak the flavour and aromatic characteristics of each type of bean.

Some people confuse strength with darkness of roast but strength depends on concentration.

# Grinding

To this day in the Middle East, pounding in a mortar, preferably wooden and with a stone pestle, is the method used to pulverize coffee. There is a beautiful song which traditionally accompanies the professional pounders, its rhythm easing the monotony of the affair. Generally, though, a long, deep groan emitted by the pounder at every blow of the heavy pestle wielded in two hands is the sound that you hear.

Brillat-Savarin, experimenting with pure Mocha beans, took it upon himself to establish which method, grinding or pounding, was to be preferred. He tasted coffee made with equal quantities of the two, and also submitted them to eminent connoisseurs. The unanimous verdict was that the coffee with the pounded powder was clearly superior to that made from the ground beans. Anyone is at liberty to repeat the experiment. For me, an electric grinder has proved less tiring and equally effective, though I cannot achieve as fine a pulverized flour for my Turkish coffee as my coffee shop does.

Many grinders exist on the market today, ranging from the old-fashioned hand grinders, which are coming back into fashion, to the electric ones that cut rather than grind. Most are equally efficient.

As soon as the tiny cells of fibrous tissues which make up the coffee beans are laid open, the precious aromatic oils and gases are released. Since the body and flavour of coffee are ground out, not boiled out, the quicker it is brewed after grinding, the better.

In choosing a mill, make sure that it is possible to adjust the coarseness of the grind over a fairly wide range. Most electric ones have whirling blades like a blender, and the degree of fineness is determined by the length of time the blades are allowed to cut. A few models are real mills, like electrically driven versions of hand grinders, and on these, the fineness is set by turning a wheel or screw.

The degree of fineness you want depends on your method of brewing and the length of your brewing cycle. The finer the grind, the more the coffee is exposed to the water, the greater the yield and therefore the shorter the brewing cycle required.

A *powdered* or *pulverized* coffee as fine as flour is used for Turkish coffee, where murkiness is not considered a disadvantage. It gives the maximum yield but loses some of the aroma in grinding. It is too fine for any of the other ways of making coffee.

*Very fine,* like cornmeal, is used for the *drip* and *filtration* methods when paper filters are used. The fine ground yields well and slows down the flow of water. A pulverized one would clog the filter. Any murkiness is banished from the liquor by the filter. It is also used for the Italian *espresso*, though small stovetop *espresso* machines, such as the 'Moka Express', work better with a very slightly coarser grind. Like powdered coffee, a very fine grind is more economical because of its high yield.

*Fine,* like granulated sugar, is used for *drip pots,* the French press or plunger (cafetière) and the Italian *Napoletana* pot with small perforations in the filter. It is also used in the vacuum method.

*Medium* is for coffee made in *the jug* by steeping to ensure that only a clear liquor is strained into the cups. More is needed, as the oils are less accessible to the water and the yield is smaller but the aroma has equally been better preserved for the brew. This grind is also used for the *pumping percolator* where a thinner grind would pass through the holes of the filter, and where the water has as much as seven or eight minutes to extract the maximum body from the coffee. Because of the weak extraction it is the least economical grind.

Although more of the aroma is lost to the air while grinding more finely, as far as storage is concerned, deterioration is faster in the coarser grind because of the ventilation. The finer the grind, the closer the particles pack together, the less the air can circulate through the mass, the less then the oxidation and the loss of aroma.

## Decaffeinated Coffee

The market for decaffeinated coffees is ever growing, with greater demands for quality and variety. Caffeine is removed from beans in the green state by either a solvent or a water method, and the taste inevitably suffers. In some of the worst of the decaffeinated coffees much of the aromatic and flavouring constituents have also disappeared with the caffeine, and even the best never have the wonderful flavour of the real thing.

In the solvent method, green beans are usually steamed to soften them and open their pores, then soaked in the solvent that dissolves the caffeine. The solvent is removed and the caffeine is kept for medicinal use and soft drinks. The beans are steamed again to remove the solvent residues, then dried. Since 1975, following a scare that the solvent trichloroethylene could cause cancer, manufacturers have generally used methylene chloride, which has not been linked with any disease. However, the European Community will be banning it from 1995 because it contributes to the depletion of the ozone layer; it will be replaced by other environmentally safe solvents. Several plants have already switched to ethyl acetate, a solvent obtained from fruit. Because this is organic, the process is called 'natural'.

In a method in which the solvent never touches the beans, these are soaked in hot water for several hours until they release the caffeine and coffee oils. The soaking water is run into another tank and combined with a solvent which absorbs the caffeine. The solvent is then separated out and the water with the coffee oils is returned to the beans so they can reabsorb the oils.

An entirely solvent-free method, for consumers worried about potential health hazards of even the minutest trace of solvent, is a water-only process. The green beans are soaked in very hot water, the caffeine is removed from the water by percolating it through charcoal, then the water is returned to the beans which reabsorb the flavour constituents. Another method soon to come on the market uses coffee oil to extract the caffeine. In yet another, beans are soaked in compressed carbon dioxide which in its liquid form combines with caffeine.

There is no general consensus in the trade about which method is best, although most feel that the one using methylene chloride produces the best-tasting coffee. Because it is so volatile they hold that it is unlikely that any traces could remain after roasting and brewing. It is worth noting that high roasting burns off up to half the caffeine content and that brewing by the Turkish coffee method further sublimates it.

# Artificial Flavourings and Flavoured Coffees

One of the largest new trends in the USA, particularly on the West Coast, is the ever-expanding market in flavoured coffees. These are flavoured beans or flavourings to add to coffee in the cup. One flavour company alone offers two hundred flavours. The big sellers are Vanilla, Chocolate, Amaretto, Irish Cream, Caramel, Bitter Almond, Praline, Cinnamon, Raspberry and Chocolate Mint, Coconut, Fudge and Toasted Hazelnut.

Many of the flavourings are artificial. Some are natural but are combined with an alcohol and glycerine base. Most have a chemical smell and an unpleasant after-taste. Yet the consumer response has been amazing. Opinions about flavoured coffees in the trade vary between those of purists, who will not sell them and see them as a negation of what good coffee is about and the views of those who have succumbed to selling them, maintaining that if people really enjoy something they should be allowed to have it, and that flavoured coffees provide an introduction to the quality coffee market to people who would otherwise not set foot in a speciality store.

# Additives and Substitutes

The usual reason for additives in coffee is economy. Though chicory and figs are the only two that have achieved popularity for their own sake, many others have been tried in the past.

When Frederick the Great of Prussia made coffee an expensive state monopoly in 1781, the poorer classes had either to steal or to fall back on substitutes. They tried barley, wheat, corn, chicory and dried figs, roasted and ground. In England after the Great Fire in 1666, strange substitutes appeared such as betony (the root of a plant belonging to the mint family) as well as bocket or saloop, a decoction of sassafras and sugar.

General Sherman, in his memoirs of his experiences in the American Civil War, lists substitutes for the drink which had become indispensable for the soldiers, including Indian corn, sweet potato and the seed of the okra plant.

All types of grains, as well as sugar and molasses, and even pieces of bread, roasted and ground have served as substitutes. An incredible variety of nuts, cereals and vegetables have been used at one time or another, from acorns and beans to beetroots and carrots, juniper berries and rice. Dandelion root is still used today and can be found ready-ground or in soluble form in health food shops. The list defies imagination. Apart from the caramel produced in roasting, it is a mystery to me how these substitutes could have tasted anything remotely like coffee.

A story is told of Prince Bismarck who, when in France with the Prussian army, entered a country inn one day and asked the host if he had any chicory in the house. He had.

'Bring it all then! All you have!'

'The man obeyed, and brought a full canister and a couple of small boxes, half filled with chicory.

'Are you sure this is all you have?' asked the chancellor.

'Yes, my Lord, every grain.'

'Then,' said Bismarck, 'leave this here and now go and make me a pot of coffee.'

There is a special fondness for chicory in France. Italians, Dutch and Germans like it, too, though in a lesser way. In England it is associated with the restrictive period of the last war, though some still like its slightly bitter taste, which they have acquired in those years. It is used in the catering trade to make coffee go further by giving it more colour and body.

The use of chicory originated in Holland in 1770. Chicory, succory or *Cichorium intybus* is a perennial plant which grows to a height of about three feet and bears pretty little blue flowers. Its leaves make a lovely salad. The long tap root is cut into slices, dried in a kiln then roasted and ground in the same way as coffee. Use about 20 per cent chicory with your coffee if you wish to make your own mixture.

Another addition which is rapidly becoming popular in this country is dried figs. This combination is now mass-produced and known as Viennese coffee.

# Instant Coffee

'Nescafé no es café (Nescafé is not coffee) is a slogan for purists in Mexico, where soluble coffee has become the trendy drink, a curious phenomenon which has overtaken many of the countries where people have a coffee tree in their back garden. Nevertheless, instant coffee is usually made with real coffee and with coffee alone. Soluble coffee, with its unvarying taste, quickness of preparation and no grounds, came into its own during the First World War, when it was shipped in large quantities to the American forces serving in Europe.

It is in the dry soluble extracts that the poorer grades from Brazil and the *robustas* from Africa and elsewhere find oblivion. Although manufacturers, whether in the multi-national brands or in the private label coffees, have made great efforts towards improving and offering different flavours and roasts, none has yet been able to capture the fine aroma nor the unique subtleties of flavour of freshly made coffee.

---

*Four*

---

# The
# Perfect Cup

---

# Brewing

In 1845 Eliza Acton wrote: 'There is no beverage which is held in more universal esteem than good coffee and none in this country at least which is obtained with greater difficulty. We hear constant and well founded complaints from foreigners and English people of the wretched compounds so commonly served up here under its name.'

When I wrote the first edition of this book a coffee man, head of one of the most important firms of mass-produced coffees, once confided to me that he usually started his lectures to Women's Institutes with the phrase, 'Not one of you can make coffee properly!' followed by the questions, 'Which one of you warms the pot? Which one waits the full

four minutes for the coffee to brew?' He played on the lack of confidence which spoils coffee-making for the great majority, trying to put the blame on others for the mediocrity of his coffee.

Things have changed in the last seventeen years, but unfortunately coffee making is still enveloped by a mystique which makes it appear more difficult than it is. There is nothing mysterious about making coffee. Indeed it could not be more simple. You can make it like tea by pouring nearly boiling water over it then straining it into a cup. Israelis pour boiling water over pulverized coffee in a cup, add a little sugar and drink it, leaving the grounds clinging to the bottom of the cup. It is called botz and it is perfectly good and as easy as instant coffee.

But as coffee lovers know, coffee has to be made with love and respect for it to live up to its aromatic and flavoursome promise. Various methods find advocates, for reasons of taste, culture, habit and lifestyle. Each method achieves a certain distinctive character. It is worth trying them all to discover your preference before becoming a victim of habit. Nor is there anything wrong in developing a taste for one particular style. Familiarity can develop the ritual of brewing to a fine art.

As far as public drinking is concerned, espresso coffee is probably the most popular type of coffee in the world now for its distinctive intense flavour, while the French press or plunger method (the cafetière) is probably the most popular way of making coffee at home.

There is an extraordinary variety of equipment and machinery available on the market, but none is essential to make an excellent coffee with fully developed flavour, aroma, strength and body. All you may need is a jug or a saucepan. However, there are some very efficient and attractive pots and devices about, each providing a brew that varies slightly from that of the others.

Coffee does not need to be cooked. The roaster has already 'cooked' it and developed the aromatic constituents sufficiently so that they are ready to be dissolved in hot water when the cells of the beans have been thoroughly opened by grinding. All that is required from brewing is to extract the already cooked aromatic constituents from the surrounding fibrous tissue. This may be perfectly well achieved by the short contact of boiling water with coffee.

Brewing is a matter of either boiling or infusion, and all the innumerable devices for making coffee, including steeping, filtration, pumping percolation, vacuum and pressure, work on these two basic principles.

With infusion, boiling water, which has cooled slightly as it is poured, extracts the caffeine and the aromatic constituents without driving away the aroma. Provided that overextraction does not occur through reheating or overheating or allowing the grounds to stand in the liquor for too long, the bitter and astringent components of roasted coffee will be left undissolved in the grounds. This method preserves the utmost aroma for the cup and obtains the maximum and purest flavour.

When coffee is boiled, there is a certain decomposition and some of the less soluble materials of an astringent and more bitter nature are dissolved, while much of the aroma (the caffeol) is steam-distilled from the brew. Many people, however, are addicted to coffee made in this way. Bitterness, an acquired taste, is also one of the basic natural tastes of coffee. When it is strong it gives an extra kick to the stimulating brew, one which perhaps makes up for the loss of some of the aroma. Admittedly, in many of the countries where coffee is boiled, the bitterness is usually mitigated by sugar and often by the perfume of spices, and of course only a little is drunk at a time, in very small cups.

In America many coffee-drinking households persist in using the much criticized but ubiquitous pumping percolator which boils the liquor continuously for several minutes.

Apart from the bitterness resulting from overextraction, which may be unpleasant for many people, there is the special tang obtained from the strong flavour of high roasted beans. There is also the more attractive bitterness of strong coffee, which is simply a concentration of the normal bitter taste, as in the French 'demitasse' and the Italian 'ristretto'. The strength of a brew depends, of course, on the amount of coffee used. The required amount is a matter of taste and is also related to the method of brewing and the fineness of grind, since the finer the grind and the longer the brewing cycle the greater the yield. Coffee might be too weak as a result of the grind being too coarse, the extraction time too short or the water not being hot enough. American experts have established that a perfect brew contains soluble solids at 19 per cent (of its own weight) of extraction. More than that results in bitterness. This perfect brew is easily obtained by following good brewing practices.

To make a perfect cup of coffee some general points are important. Cold, freshly drawn water must be used, the purer and the softer the better. Any salts or chemicals in it will spoil the taste.

The grind must be of the right fineness for the chosen method.

The pot must be warmed.

When making an infusion, the water *must* come into contact with the ground coffee at *just under boiling point* to extract the oils and aromatic principles from the cells.

Always make coffee at full strength, as there is nothing more insipid than a weak diluted drink. As a general rule, with a fine grind you will need one rounded tablespoon of ground coffee to a coffee-cupful (about 210 ml, 7½ fl oz, 1 cup) of water. I like it extra strong and use a rounded tablespoon to 150–175 ml, 5 or 6 fl oz, ¾ cup of water. If you want a double strength 'demitasse', use one rounded tablespoon to half the quantity of water (about 125 ml, 4 fl oz, ½ cup). If you are using a coarser grind, you may need as much as four rounded tablespoons to 600 ml (1 pint, 2½ cups) of water. The quantity of coffee required varies a little according to the method, since the longer the water is allowed to act on the coffee, the less is needed. Also, the finer the grind, the greater the yield, the less coffee required. Ultimately, of course, personal taste dictates the strength or weakness of the perfect cup. For a weaker infusion, do not use less grounds with the usual amount of water, as this results in overextraction of the less pleasant, more bitter and woody elements of the bean. Make it regular strength, and dilute it. For the same reason do not use less of a high yielding (such as pulverized) grind with a longer brewing cycle.

Drink the coffee hot, as soon as it is made. An hour later it will have lost its aroma. Reheat coffee if necessary *au bain marie*, in a saucepan of boiling water, and not by bringing it to the boil. Some people like to keep black coffee hot in a Thermos flask.

Keep coffee covered if you are going to drink it later. Not all metals are suitable for brewing, as coffee liquor reacts chemically with some, affecting the taste of the coffee. Iron and aluminium should be avoided. Silver, tinned copper, enamelled iron and stainless steel may be used without any risk of contamination. Otherwise earthenware and glass make the best containers. Although aluminium is often used, it does give an odd aftertaste.

And, of course, never re-use coffee grounds; and do wash your equipment well, as grounds and oils soon become rancid.

## INFUSIONS

Various ways of making a simple infusion find the most favour with coffee lovers all over the world. Steeping the grounds in water just under boiling point, v thout further boiling, preserves the utmost aroma and flavour without allowing a trace of bitterness. The plunger pot, drip, filter and jug methods work on the same principle.

The idea first appeared in France in 1711 for making coffee *sans ébullition* (without boiling) in the form of a cloth bag containing grounds dropped inside the coffee pot over which boiling water is poured – a device still in use in many countries. Its main drawback is that keeping the bag clean and hygienic requires a great deal of attention. It must be washed and left in fresh water until it is used again.

## IN A JUG

So like brewing tea, this manner was once the most popular in England.

Warm the pot by scalding. Measure the required amount of medium-ground coffee into the pot. Use at least four heaped tablespoons for 600 ml (1 pint, 2½ cups) of water. Pour on nearly boiling water and stir thoroughly with a wooden spoon. Keeping the pot warm under a tea-cosy, allow the coffee to stand for four to six minutes. Pour through a strainer taking care not to disturb the grounds which have settled at the bottom of the jug.

## THE PLUNGER (CAFETIÈRE)

The French press or plunger pot (cafetière) works on the same principle as the jug (previous page) but with an inside strainer in the form of a fine-mesh filter plunger unit attached to the lid. In very few years it has become the most popular home-brewing device on the market. Little pots for one first made their appearance in French restaurants. In fine heat-resistant glass with a silver or gold frame (there are also plastic ones), they are very attractive to bring to the table and extremely simple to use.

*Method:* Heat the glass beaker by scalding. Put in the required amount of fine ground coffee, add nearly boiling water and stir. Allow to steep for four minutes, stir again then push the plunger filter down gently with the lid as far as it will go, pushing the grounds to the bottom of the beaker.

You can find large ones which serve twelve to eighteen cups.

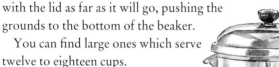

### THE DRIP POT

In 1800, the Archbishop of Paris, Jean Baptiste de Belloy, devised a pot which is still today the model for many a drip pot (called *'percolateur'* in France). It was given the accolade by Brillat-Savarin. Many drip pots exist. Most are in three parts. The top receives the water, a bottom pot receives the coffee and there is a coffee basket in between the two.

Porcelain ones are the best and the most used, but there are also silver and aluminium ones. These have the disadvantage of allowing more heat loss, and aluminium leaves an aftertaste. However, unlike porcelain ones they can be kept warm on a hotplate while the coffee drips.

*Method:* Preheat the pot by scalding with hot water. Measure the necessary amount of medium ground coffee into the filter section (perforated chinaware or metal). Pour the required amount of fresh boiling water into the upper container, then cover. When all the liquid has dripped through, remove the upper section and serve.

*Café filtre,* individual drips placed over a cup in French cafés, are often slow to run through and need some encouragement by applying pressure with the palm of the hand if they are to fill the cup before the coffee is cold.

## THE NEAPOLITAN MACHINETTA

This two-tiered pot, for years found only in aluminium, is also made in stainless steel. There are three parts: a cylinder base with a handle is the bottom part, another cylinder with an upside down pouring spout screws on top, and a small coffee basket fits between them.

*Method:* Pour water in the base. Fill the strainer basket loosely with fine ground coffee and place it over the base then screw on the upper part. Put the pot to boil over a flame. When steam comes out from a tiny hole in the lower part of the machinetta turn it over so that it is upside down. The boiling water drips through the coffee into the part with the spout. When it has all gone through, it is ready to serve.

## THE FILTER

In this form of the drip method, a cone-shaped paper filter bag removes all traces of the slightest sediment, resulting in a perfectly clear, flavoursome liquor. A fine grind which gives a maximum yield should be used. Pulverized coffee would clog the filter and stop the flow of liquor and a coarse grind would let the water run through too quickly and make for a weak brew. Individual filters are available for single cups. Larger ones fit over jugs. Coffee correctly brewed in this way is unfailingly clear, fragrant and seductive – but the device must be properly handled. A variety of automatic coffee-makers use this method.

*Method:* Preheat the pot by scalding. Insert filter bag into dry filter. Measure fine ground coffee into filter (one measuring spoon, usually

provided with the device, per cup). Moisten coffee with boiling water to cover and gently shake the filter so that no dry lumps remain. Allow to steep for half a minute, then top up the filter to the required level. You can keep the heatproof jug warm during the filtering on a hotplate.

## THE VACUUM OR GLASS BALLOON

This was an international favourite for a long time because of its charismatic visual appeal. The glass container exhibits the changing colours of coffee developing, adding to the pleasantly sensuous ritual of making coffee at the table. Its reputation has, unfortunately been somewhat tarnished by the many restaurants and hotels in the sixties and seventies that used the device to make coffee in advance and warm it up before serving. Robert Napier, a Scottish marine engineer, invented the first model in 1840, an extraordinary device with a magical-looking silver globe, a syphon, a strainer and a mixing bowl.

*Method:* Pour the necessary amount of fresh cold water into the lower bowl and place on heat. Place filter into upper funnel and add the measured quantity of medium fine or fine coffee. Place over the lower bowl and twist to seal tightly. Place on heat and bring to the boil. When the water has risen into the funnel, stir the coffee and water mixture well. When it has ceased to rise, leave on the heat a further minute, then turn off. When all the coffee, has filtered down into the lower bowl, remove the funnel and serve.

### THE PUMPING PERCOLATOR

A device that made its appearance in 1825 and enjoyed a certain vogue through the nineteenth century is the one that finds the least favour today. A weak infusion liquor is boiled and recirculated by the pumping action of steam until a satisfactory degree of extraction has been reached. The continuous boiling produces a certain bitterness. The main advantage is that it requires less coffee, since the water acts on it for a longer time. Although it is still used in the majority of American coffee-drinking homes, this method has become the target for the anger of the trade, who blame it for the declining sales of the last decade.

*Method:* Pour the required amount of fresh cold water into the percolator. When the water boils, remove from the heat. Measure the required amount of medium-ground coffee into the basket and insert the basket into the percolator. Cover, return to the heat and allow to percolate gently for six to eight minutes. Remove the basket with the grounds and serve.

## TURKISH COFFEE

The 'black mud' sucked by the Levantines prevails throughout the Middle East up to Greece, North Africa and the Balkans. As the Frenchman, Thevenot, already wrote in the seventeenth century: 'One must drink it hot, but in several instalments, otherwise it is no good. One takes it in little swallows for fear of burning one's self – in such fashion that in a *cavekane* (café) one hears a pleasant little musical sucking sound.' He was talking of the Turkish version of Arab coffee which was originated in the early sixteenth century, adding sugar and just bringing it to the boil three times, instead of boiling for a long time.

The orientalist Richard Burton describes the use of ambergris in coffee in *Love, War and Fancy.*

'The egesta of the whale, found in lumps weighing several pounds in the sea on the coast of Zanzibar, is sold at a high price being held a potent aphrodisiac. A small hollow is drilled in the bottom of the cup and the coffee is poured upon the bit of ambergris it contains; when the oleaginous matter shows in dots amidst the *kaymagh* (coffee cream), the bubbly froth which floats upon the surface, an expert "coffee servant" distributes it equally among the guests.'

I personally have not seen anyone flavouring with ambergris, whereas I have seen many using cardamom, cinnamon, nutmeg and cloves. Cardamom is particularly popular, dropped into the pot while it is boiling. Some people open the pod, extract one seed and use this alone in the coffee.

*Method:* Make it in an *ibrik* (or *kanaka*), a smallish long-handled metal pot made of tinned copper or brass. If one is not available, use a small saucepan. *Ibriks* come in various sizes. The number of coffees they will

make is often scratched on the underside. If you do not know, measure
the capacity with small coffee cups. Beans should be roasted medium
high or continental and ground to a fine powder.

*For two coffees:*
2 very heaped teaspoons of pulverized coffee
2 very heaped teaspoons of sugar or to taste
2 small coffee cups of water

Boil the water with the sugar in the *ibrik*. Add the coffee, stir well and
return to the fire. When the coffee froths up to the rim, remove from the
fire. Repeat twice again. Some let a drop of cold water precipitate the
grounds; others rap the pot smartly; others still let them settle by waiting.
  You might like to add spices. Try one at a time. Put them in the *ibrik*
to boil with the water. Try a cardamom pod, a couple of cloves, a small
stick of cinnamon or a pinch of freshly grated nutmeg.
  Serve as soon as the grounds have settled while still hot. Pour or rather
shake out a little froth for each cup. Some grounds will settle at the bottom
of the cup. You are not supposed to eat them. As Dufour said, 'In the
Levant it is only the scum of the people who swallow the grounds.' But you
can make use of them. Some people, usually women, profess to be able
to read fortunes in the trickle of the grounds in an upturned cup. Grounds
also have medicinal value, properties which have been borne out in
scientific research; deodorant, antiseptic, germicidal and bactericidal.

I am tempted to relate a scatological anecdote which illustrates the double virtue of spent grounds.

'A man went to see his doctor complaining of haemorrhoids. The doctor advised him to drink coffee six or seven times a day and each time to go and wash the painful parts and rub them well with the grounds left at the bottom of the cup. After a week of applying the cure assiduously, the patient returned to his doctor who asked him to remove his trousers and to bend down. Taking a close look and after due reflection, the doctor said with tredpidation: "I can see a tall young blonde coming into your life".'

## STOVE-TOP MOKA ESPRESSO

Espresso is one of the best-loved types of coffee. This simple way of making it works on the same steam pressure principle as some of the big machines and is almost as effective. In these machines the water vapour that is created just before boiling is forced through the ground coffee and into an upper reservoir where it condenses back into liquid and from where it can be served. On account of the pressure, the water boils at a higher temperature than normal. Steam is forced through the grounds, extracting more than boiling water normally does.

The stove-top pot is in two parts, screwed together with a filter funnel in the middle. The original brand was called Moka Express and was made in aluminium which gives an unpleasant taste. There are now many rivals in many sizes and mostly made of stainless steel.

*Method:* Fill the base with enough water to reach the safety valve. Fill the filter funnel with finely ground coffee without pressing the coffee down. Place the funnel loosely on the base and screw the top firmly to the base. Place over heat. As soon as the coffee begins to rise to the top through the stem, lower the heat to a minimum. A gurgling noise indicates that all the water in the lower part has risen through the grounds. Remove from heat. When the coffee stops rising it is ready to serve.

The rubber washer needs replacing occasionally, and remember not to leave the pot over heat when there is no water left in the base. If you leave the pot unused for more than a few days, scrub it with hot water and a stiff brush before using it again.

### ESPRESSO CULTURE

Espresso coffee is one much cherished aspect of Italian culture which has conquered the world much like pizza. Cafés all over Europe now are fitted with espresso machines which make exquisite coffee. Recently the espresso machine has taken America by storm with its shiny stylish machinery and accessories, its techniques, rituals and styles of drinking, attendant ideologies, menu lists and jargon – they talk of *ristretto* and *doppio, latte macchiatto* and *crema*. Most of all it is the rediscovered appeal of the splendid aromatic, syrupy concentrated taste and creamy heaviness of espresso and the delicate clouds of milk foam floating on top of cappuccinos that have caused its renaissance.

Espresso's place is in the café world of public drinking. The original espresso machine was invented in the mid-nineteenth century in France and was exhibited at the Exposition de Paris in 1855. It was a monster of a machine designed for commercial use – to brew coffee instantaneously under the pressure of steam. It was adopted by various Italian makers who developed the idea. After World War II Gaggia brought out a model in which a spring-powered piston pumped by a handle pushed the hot water through the coffee. Later button-operated machines worked with simple hydraulic pumps. These days the process is entirely automated and includes milk-frothing equipment by which compressed steam is forced through cold milk from a nozzle, heating it and producing a light foam. But the operation is still enveloped by ritual mystique.

Many people want to reproduce the appealing tastes of the café quality espresso in their own homes but it often remains an unattainable goal. There is a great number of different home espresso makers at a wide range of prices on the market, all of which work in different ways and with varying results. In all of them the principle is the same: hot water is forced rapidly with great pressure through ground coffee directly into coffee cups so that there is maximum extraction of the flavour components in the shortest possible time but with none of the unpleasant elements. They work by different processes: by the action of trapped steam, by means of a pump or with a lever-controlled piston. These last two are the more expensive machines but they do produce a richer, smoother drink of near-café quality. They also have a valve for frothing and heating milk. It is important to find out the merits and weaknesses of each before investing. But all these machines need to be properly handled to produce the much-loved rich and aromatic coffee with syrupy body and most desirable light brown foam called *crema*. They all require patience and practice until you get the feel of it – in other words the coffee has to be made with love.

Here are some recommendations for best results. Coffee must be very finely ground. You may like to use the traditional southern Italian dark roast which produces a distinctive bitter kick or you may prefer a medium roast used by northern Italians. The grounds must not be packed too tightly in the *gruppa* – the metal filter cup that holds them – or the water will not get through properly, nor too lightly or the result will be watered down and insipid. Don't try to get more coffee liquor out of the grounds; overextracted coffee is thin and bitter.

**Espresso** is strong and concentrated, has the bittersweet bite of a dark roast and concentrated liquor. It can only be drunk black in small quantities and sweetened. It can be served with a thin cut slice of lemon hung on the side of the cup.

**Caffe latte** is a half and half mixture of espresso and hot milk. Milk mellows the strong sharp taste of the coffee.

**Cappuccino** is one third espresso with one third hot milk topped with one third foam. Sprinkle if you like with powdered or shaved bitter chocolate or with cinnamon or nutmeg and serve it with sugar. The word cappuccino is derived from the colour of the habit worn by Capuchin monks.

A few years ago in Sardinia, I was eating lunch in an out of the way seaside restaurant. The owner came to ask me where I was from, then asked, 'Why do English people ask for cappuccino with spaghetti Bolognese?' All the locals stopped eating to listen to my explanation of the social history of coffee bars in Britain offering spaghetti with cappuccino. Italians only drink it for breakfast. In America, too, people generally prefer to drink their espresso cut with milk.

# Black Coffee

For the purist, the only way to drink coffee is black, or *nature* as the French call it. Across the Channel that usually means very strong, from a high roast, sometimes burnt almost to a char, and served *en demitasse*, the traditional small after-dinner cup.

For *café nature* use one heaped tablespoon of ground coffee to each 120 ml (4 fl oz, ½ cup) of water. The higher yield of the Italian espresso method results in the extra strong *ristretto*. *Lungo* is their weaker version, served in larger cups.

Serve it very hot as soon as it is made. Drink it sensitively like wine, appreciating the bouquet and the colour. It is not affectation but simply making the most of what is good.

### A NOTE ON FLAVOURING

Coffee has made some successful marriages of flavour, some no doubt by happy chance, which are well worth trying out. A pleasant sensation for the palate is the use of lemon in coffee.

In Italy and many other parts of the world, a strip of lemon peel is often curled round the rim of the cup. You may add excitement to your drink with a sprinkling of grated lemon or orange peel, or, as in the old Russian way, with a squeeze of lemon juice.

Moroccans like to use whole black peppercorns to give extra kick. They may add a pinch of salt, a habit also popular in Ethiopia, to bring out the finer flavours. As Simone Beck points out, 'The flavour of even the finest coffee will be enhanced if at the moment of pouring boiling water over the coffee, one adds a tiny pinch of salt.'

# Coffee with Milk

Inspired by the drinking of tea with milk, Nieuhoff, the Dutch Ambassador to China, was officially the first person to try coffee with milk, around 1660.

The French breakfast drink *café au lait* is traditionally served in large bowls on which you can warm your hands, or in cups large enough to dip a piece of *baguette*, a *croissant* or a *brioche*. Hot milk and extra-strong coffee are poured from two pots simultaneously into the cup. Proportions vary from half-and-half to one part milk and three parts coffee. It is for you to decide how you like it.

In Vienna, whose coffee has been described as without equal, two parts of coffee to one of hot milk is called *melange* and topped with whipped cream. *Brauner* coffee is darker and *schwarzer* is without milk.

In Italy equal parts of hot milk and espresso make *caffè latte*, while cappuccino is topped with frothy milk. *Espresso macchiato* is espresso coffee with a little frothy milk on top. *Latte macchiato* is espresso poured over hot frothy milk. All these may have a little grated chocolate, cinnamon, nutmeg or grated orange zest sprinkled on top.

## Café Borgia or Viennese Coffee
## with Chocolate

A delicious alternative to *café au lait* relies on the special affinity of the sister berries, chocolate and coffee. The alliance usually termed Mocha, after the coffee's first port of export, is variously interpreted and exotically named Café Borgia, Viennese Coffee, Javanese Hot Mocha and Mexican Negrita.

This can be made with plain, or better still, bitter chocolate, powdered drinking chocolate or cocoa powder.

To make four delicious cups, gently melt 100 g (4 oz, 1 cup) of chocolate in a saucepan, being careful not to burn it. Add sugar or honey to taste and stir in four tablespoons of cream. Pour in four cupfuls of hot, freshly made coffee a little at a time, beating well till frothy. Keep hot over a small fire. Serve with whipped cream and sprinkle with a little ground cinnamon, cocoa or grated orange peel. A spiced version uses four cloves and a stick of cinnamon brewed with the coffee and strained or filtered with the grounds. If you are making one cup only, it may be easier to use powdered drinking chocolate. Some, such as Brazilians, like to pour hot milk on the chocolate and add it to an equal quantity of strong hot coffee. A Javanese Mocha is sometimes topped with marshmallow cream.

Whatever it is called, I suspect the marriage of coffee and chocolate originates in Mexico, where the Spanish Conquistadores first found Montezuma's courtiers drinking cups of chocolate. For their 'Negrita', Mexicans brew coffee with the usual spices, beat it with an equal quantity of strong cocoa and serve it with whipped cream.

## Laced Coffee

An excellent after-dinner habit is to take coffee laced with a spirit or a liqueur. The French *cordial* or the Italian *corretto*, equally good at other times of the day, is said even by the puritanical to aid digestion. Others simply love it. Fill a small cup only three-quarters full of strong hot black coffee. Sweeten it if you like and add a jigger or a dash of a favourite spirit.

You need not use the élite of spirits. An *eau de vie* from the local cottage industry, distilled from any fruit, is likely to be as good.

In Normandy, Calvados, a distilled cider from local apples, is poured into a half-full cup of coffee to fill it to the brim. In the South of France, Marc, a spirit made from grape skins and pips, is drunk with coffee, also in equal quantities. Poire is a Belgian favourite, and in Switzerland, Kirsch made of cherry stones. Other *alcools blancs* made of apricots, blue plums, raspberries and strawberries are excellent. Cognac and Armagnac are extravagant but great.

Rum is magnificent in coffee and, of course, Tia Maria, the coffee
liqueur, is a natural companion.

The fondness for alcohol in coffee is not confined to Europe. Laced
coffees are also very popular in the Americas. Here, cream, thick and
heavy or whipped and light, is an added delight to the rum and to the
numerous fruit and other liqueurs of South America.

## Irish Coffee

Into a warmed, large wineglass put two jiggers of Irish whiskey and one
teaspoon or more of sugar to taste. Pour in freshly made hot coffee and
stir. As the contents revolve, add a jigger of double (heavy) cream, drib-
bling it slowly over the back of a spoon into the drink. Allow the cream
to float to the top and do not stir.

## Café Brûlot Diabolique

This punch can be made in a saucepan, but a chafing dish or a silver bowl
at the table and elusive flames in the darkness provide a fitting sense of
drama. The quantities I give will serve about six to eight people. Make
900 ml/1½ pints/3¾ cups of coffee and keep it hot. In a deep silver bowl
put eight cloves, one cinnamon stick, the peels of an orange and of a
lemon cut in a thin ribbon and sugar to taste. Heat 150 ml/¼ pint/
⅔ cup) of brandy, a ladle at a time, ignite and pour over the ingredients
in the bowl. Stir to dissolve the sugar. Pour in the hot coffee slowly and
stir gently until the flames fade. You may also add a ladle of flaming
Cointreau at this stage. Ladle the *café brûlot* into small, warmed cups.

# Iced Coffee

Having recently experienced Athens' hottest day for many years, I
emerged convinced that few drinks are as refreshing as iced coffee.

The innumerable versions served up throughout the world reveals a
shadowiness of boundaries between the *cafés glacés*, the *refrescos de café*,
the *frappés*, milk shakes, 'frosts', 'froths', 'floats' and 'nectars'. Chilled
coffee can be served on ice cubes or with crushed ice or ice cream, and
can be topped with whipped cream. Mixed with cream, which enhances
iced coffee more than milk does, it is the celebrated *café Liégeois*.

Ways of making iced coffee are numerous, and in each case the same is
true – that to make good iced coffee you must first make good hot

coffee. Do not make it too long in advance (three hours at most); sweeten it or not, and simply allow it to cool in the refrigerator in a glass or china jug, covered to preserve as much of the aroma possible, and so that it does not pick up any alien odour. If you will be using ice cubes which dilute the drink, make your coffee double strength using half the usual amount of water for the same amount of ground coffee. Allow this to cool, but not for too long, then pour it into a glass filled with an equal quantity of ice cubes. Ice cubes made by pouring fresh coffee into freezer trays add coolness without diluting the drink. Long glasses are attractive for serving.

Suitable additions include a strip or two of lemon peel. Fresh mint is also an excellent flavouring for cold coffee. Drop in a few leaves straight from your garden while the brew is cooling. Angostura bitters, popular in Italy, add a provocative taste, and rum is delightful too, as Brazilians well know. Pour a little into the chilled coffee just as you are about to serve it. And of course there are all the aromatic and the traditional companions; chocolate, honey and coconut, which are as good with cold as with hot coffee. A scoop of ice cream – vanilla, coffee or chocolate – will usually enhance any iced coffee.

## Iced Coffee with Milk
*Café au lait* or Viennese Coffee may be put to cool in the refrigerator, covered – sweetened if you like. Serve topped with whipped cream. A little single (light) cream may be preferred to milk. Otherwise, prepare double strength coffee and beat well with chilled milk in equal parts just before serving.

## Iced Spiced Coffee
For a largish quantity make about 1 litre/1¾ pints/4⅓ cups of strong fresh coffee. Drop in four cinnamon sticks, eight cloves and eight all-spice berries to steep while it cools, covered, in the refrigerator for at least an hour. Strain and serve over ice cubes. Sweeten to taste and garnish with whipped cream.

## Iced Coffee with Honey
Pour freshly made strong coffee over a glassful of ice cubes with honey to taste (about a tablespoon will usually do). Top with whipped cream and dust with cinnamon and grated nutmeg.

### Iced Coffee Mocha

Pour 1 litre/1¾ pints/4⅓ cups of freshly made hot coffee over 100 g/ 4 oz/1 cup of chocolate (warmed up and melted in a saucepan), a little at first and beating well until it is dissolved. Sweeten if you like, then chill. Garnish with whipped cream and chocolate dust or shavings.

### Iced Coffee Cocktail

Make 1 litre/1¾ pints/4⅓ cups of coffee and let it cool in a covered glass or china jug in the refrigerator with a long strip of lemon peel. Before serving, stir in a jigger or two of Crème de Cacao or Cognac. Pour into wine glasses over crushed ice or ice cubes with sugar to taste, or honey if you prefer. Dribble about a tablespoon of fresh cream off the back of a spoon into each glass.

### Cognac Mocha

A delicious iced mixture of equal parts of very strong coffee, milk and Cognac, is French.

# Cafés Frappés

*Frappés* are made with ice in a liquidizer, and blended until the texture is smooth, creamy and frothy. A lot of ice is used, sometimes as much ice as coffee. The coffee must be made strong accordingly, one-and-a-half times as strong or even double strength, that is, using half the usual quantity of water in brewing, so that it will not be too weak when combined with ice. Use a good blend for a flavoursome coffee. Sugar may be added, according to taste. Fresh cream or ice cream are especially good blended into the *frappé* when the ice is already crushed. Serve the *frappé* immediately after it is made, as the froth soon subsides. If you like, top it with whipped cream.

### Spiced Coffee Frappé

Pour 600 ml/1 pint/2½ cups of freshly brewed, extra strong coffee into a jug over two cinnamon sticks, four cloves and four allspice berries, cover and leave for at least one hour to cool in the refrigerator. Strain into a liquidizer, add a 150 ml/¼ pint/⅔ cup of cream and about six ice cubes. Blend to a creamy froth and serve immediately. In the same way, make honey, maple syrup or butterscotch *frappés* by adding any of these in the liquidizer. Omit the spices.

### Rum and Coffee Frappé

Alcohol adds excitement to many *frappés*. This one is delicious. Blend 600 ml/1 pint/2½ cups of chilled extra strong coffee with four ice cubes, three tablespoons of sugar or honey and three tablespoons of dark rum. When the ice is well crushed, add 150 ml/¼ pint/⅔ cup of vanilla ice cream, blend a few seconds more, and serve immediately.

### Café Alexander

This is another very pleasant mixture. Pour 600 ml/1 pint/2½ cups of extra strong chilled coffee into a liquidizer with three to four tablespoons of sugar, 150 ml/¼ pint/⅔ cup of cream and three tablespoons each of brandy and Crème de Cacao liqueur. Drop in about six ice cubes and blend to a frothy cream. Serve at once.

### Moka Helado

Pour 400 ml/¾ pint/2 cups of hot freshly made coffee over 75 g/3 oz/ ¾ cup of chocolate (warmed and slightly melted). Pour a little at first and beat well to dissolve the chocolate properly. Chill, covered, in your refrigerator. Just before serving, combine in a blender with 300 ml/ ½ pint/1¼ cups of vanilla or coffee ice cream, and some sugar if you like. Serve at once.

### Coffee Rumba

Blend 400 ml/¾ pint/2 cups of chilled coffee in a liquidizer with 300 ml/ ½ pint/1¼ cups of coffee ice cream, three to four tablespoons of rum and sugar to taste. Blend quickly and serve at once sprinkled with grated nutmeg. This is also good with Angostura bitters instead of rum.

### Coffee Ice Cream Soda

Stir 150 ml/¼ pint/⅔ cups of fresh single (light) cream into 400 ml/ ¾ pint/2 cups of chilled, strong, sweetened coffee in a jug. Pour into tall glasses, only half filling them. Add scoops of ice cream in each glass and fill with ice-cold soda water.

# Five

# Desserts and Cakes

Coffee plays a part in a remarkable variety of sweet dishes, as do chocolate and the vanilla pod, both of which coffee often partners. A good companion to most spirits and spices, it goes well with all nuts, especially with caramelized and crushed pralines. It gives a subtle surprise flavour to a few sauces and syrups for fruits such as baked apples, fried bananas and stewed pears, or served with ice creams, mousses, puddings and souffles. Various creams and custards find an original alternative with the addition of a little coffee. Many dishes have evolved around the special qualities of coffee and these often go under the name of Mocha.

'Sorbet' and 'sherbet' are derived from the Arabic word, *sharbat*, for cold drink. Water ices are the most fragrant and delightful of foods to have been used as appetizers and digestives. They are still the interim course for soothing and revitalizing the stomachs of gourmands at London *barmitzvahs*, as they were at the feasts of ancient Rome. The history of water ices starts in the third century B.C. in China; they have come to us via the Arabs through Renaissance Italy.

## Granita al Caffé

*Granita al caffé con panna montata* (with whipped cream) has remained the speciality of Italy, where people pour their sweetened left-over coffee into the freezer as soon as they have had enough. To make it, all you need is coffee, preferably a darkish roast, and sugar. However, mixing in a little egg white whipped to a firm snow makes for a less gritty consistency.

SERVES 10

75–100 g/3–4 oz/1 cup finely ground coffee
200–250 g/7–8 oz/2 cups sugar
1.2 litres/2 pints/5 cups water
1 egg white, stiffly beaten.

I like to use the greater quantity of coffee. The large amount of sugar is necessary, as otherwise the ice is hard and coarse. Put the water and sugar in a saucepan. Boil for a few minutes. Add the ground coffee to the boiling hot syrup and leave to infuse for ten minutes. Strain through a fine sieve, and cool. When it is cold, pour into a covered ice tray in the freezer. When it is partly frozen, turn it into a bowl, beat in the stiffly whisked egg white and return to the ice tray. Freeze until firm and smooth, beating every half-hour to break up the ice granules.

You may serve with whipped cream. The use of a churn freezer will of course result in a smoother texture.

 ESSERTS AND CAKES

## Parfait au Café
Light and creamy and as perfect as the name implies.

SERVES 6

4 heaped tablespoons freshly roasted medium
ground coffee
300 ml/½ pint/1¼ cups single (light) cream
300 ml/½ pint/1¼ cups double (heavy) cream
4 egg yolks
150 g/5 oz/⅔ cup sugar

Bring the single (light) cream almost to the boil. Add the coffee, stir well and let it infuse for at least twenty minutes. Beat the sugar and the egg yolks in a bowl. Strain the cream through a fine sieve into the egg mixture and beat vigorously until well blended. Set the pan over boiling water and stir until the mixture thickens like a custard. Leave to cool. Whip the double (heavy) cream until fairly stiff and fold into the cream custard. Freeze in an ice tray for three to four hours. Stir after an hour, bringing the frozen sides into the middle.

There are many delicious variations to this basic coffee ice cream. You may add Tia Maria or Curaçao, or you may fold in grated chocolate or a chocolate sauce. Crushed burnt almonds or *pralin* (see method, *Mocha Praliné*, page 114) made with almonds or hazelnuts may be stirred into the cooled custard before freezing. Chopped boiled chestnuts macerated in maraschino are delicious mixed into the ice cream before it is frozen. In France, scoops of these *parfaits* are often served on a bed of whipped cream and decorated with chocolate-covered coffee beans. An irresistible *coupe* called 'Jamaïque' is pineapple dice soaked in rum, covered with coffee ice and sprinkled with freshly pulverized coffee. Another, 'Clo-Clo', has broken *marrons glacés* soaked in maraschino at the bottom of the *coupe*. These are covered with coffee ice cream decorated with vanilla-flavoured whipped cream in which is embedded a single *marron*.

## Coffee Syrup

A syrup to serve with ice creams and puddings. Into a sugar syrup made by boiling 500 g/1 lb sugar and 150 ml/¼ pint/⅔ cup of water, stir two teaspoons of instant coffee and four tablespoons of cocoa, and cook a little while longer.

## Coffee Sauce

A sauce to serve with ice creams and puddings. Beat two eggs. Add 150 ml/¼ pint/⅔ cup of strong hot coffee gradually, beating well. Add a pinch of salt and 50 g/2 oz/¼ cup of sugar, and stir over boiling water until the sauce thickens. Do not let it curdle. Chill. Just before serving, fold in 150 ml/¼ pint/⅔ cup of thick whipped cream.

## ESSERTS AND CAKES

## Chocolate and Coffee Sauce

Another sauce to serve with ice creams and puddings. Melt 100 g/¼ lb of bittersweet chocolate broken into pieces in 30 ml/1 fl oz/1 tablespoon of strong coffee and and stir well. Let it cool and add 50 g/2 oz/4 tablespoons of butter, a little at a time, beating until it is thoroughly blended.

## Mocha Butter Cream

A filling for cakes. Beat two egg yolks with 75 g/3 oz/⅓ cup of icing (confectioner's) sugar in a bowl until pale and creamy. Continue to beat over boiling water until the cream has thickened. Dissolve two tablespoons of instant coffee in two tablespoons of water, milk or rum and beat well into the egg mixture. Remove from the heat. Stir in while still warm 75 g/3 oz/5 tablespoons of unsalted butter in little pieces, one at a time, beating until well blended.

## St Valentine's Cream

### SERVES 3–5

A light cream. Beat 125 g/4 oz/8 tablespoons of cream cheese with two egg yolks, two dessertspoons of sugar and the same amount of cream. Add one level tablespoon of medium roasted and pulverized fresh ground coffee or one teaspoon of instant coffee and mix well. Fold in two stiffly beaten egg whites. Serve chilled in little pots.

## Coffee Mousse

### SERVES 6

A light and fragrant dessert. Make 150 ml/¼ pint/⅔ cup of fresh, extra strong coffee using three heaped tablespoons of a medium roast. While this is still hot, stir in 15 g/½ oz/1 tablespoon of powdered unflavoured gelatine until dissolved. Beat three egg yolks with three or four tablespoons of sugar in a bowl over a pan of hot water until thick and creamy. Remove from the pan and continue to beat until it has cooled. Gradually stir in the coffee and gelatine mixture and 150 ml/¼ pint/⅔ cup of single (light) cream, and beat well. Whisk the three egg whites until they are stiff, then gently fold into the coffee mixture. Pour into a wet mould and chill until it is set.

This mousse may also be scented with a vanilla pod (bean). Other excellent alternative additions are rum, Kirsch and Cognac.

# Mocha Mousse
A chocolate mousse with a taste of coffee.

SERVES 6–8

100 g/4 oz/1 cup bitter chocolate
150 ml/¼ pint/⅔ cup water
4 tablespoons ground coffee
175 g/6 oz/¾ cup caster (superfine) sugar
5 eggs, separated
1 tablespoon Cognac or coffee liqueur

Melt the chocolate, broken into squares, in the top of a double boiler. Make a concentrated coffee with the water and coffee grounds, strain and stir in the sugar. Add this to the chocolate in the double boiler. Stir until well blended. Add the yolks, one at a time, beating vigorously. Remove from the heat quickly when the sauce thickens slightly, and add Cognac. Beat the egg whites stiff and fold into the mixture when it is only just warm. Pour into small individual bowls and chill overnight.

A delightful alternative is to stir a little *pralin* (see method, *Mocha Praliné*, page 114) into the mousse.

## Frozen Coffee Mousse Pralineé

SERVES 6–8

Make a coarsely crushed or chopped *pralin* (see *Mocha Praliné*, page 114) with blanched hazelnuts or almonds caramelized in 100 g/4 oz/ ½ cup sugar. Then make a mousse with:

4 eggs, separated
75 g/3 oz/⅓ cup caster (superfine) sugar
3 teaspoons powdered instant coffee
300 ml/½ pint/1¼ cups double (heavy) cream

Beat the yolks in a bowl until pale and creamy. Continue to beat over hot water until thickened. Stir in the instant coffee, remove from the heat and incorporate the *pralin*. Allow to cool. Whip the double (heavy) cream until firm and fold into the coffee mixture. Whip the egg whites very stiff and beat in 25 g/1 oz/2 tablespoons of sugar. Very carefully fold into the cream. Pour gently into an attractive, wetted mould and freeze for at least an hour before serving. Dip for a second into hot water and unmould. Pour a chocolate and coffee sauce (page 105) over it, and serve.

# $\mathscr{C}$OFFEE

## Bavaroise au Café

SERVES 6–8

600 ml/1 pint/2½ cups milk
5 heaped tablespoons pale roast ground coffee
5 egg yolks
100 g/4 oz/½ cup caster (superfine) sugar
15 g/½ oz/1 tablespoon gelatine
150 ml/¼ pint/⅔ cup double (heavy) cream
3 tablespoons Cognac – optional

Bring the milk to the boil. Stir in the ground coffee and leave to infuse for about twenty minutes. Strain. Whisk the eggs in a bowl. Add the sugar gradually and whisk well until pale and creamy. Slowly beat in the hot milk. Transfer to a saucepan over medium heat and stir with a wooden spoon until the mixture has thickened into a custard. Remove from the heat. Add the gelatine, dissolved in two tablespoons of hot water, and beat into the hot custard. Leave to cool a little in the refrigerator.

Beat the cream until firm and gently fold into the custard. Stir in a little Cognac if you like. Pour into a lightly oiled mould. Chill in the refrigerator for three to four hours, until firm. Unmould and serve with a chocolate sauce poured over it.

*For the sauce:* Melt 100 g/4 oz/1 cup of bitter chocolate over boiling water. Add 250 ml/9 fl oz/1 cup of cream and 75 g/3 oz/⅓ cup of caster (superfine) sugar and stir well. Flavour if you like with a little vanilla, a quarter-teaspoon of cinnamon or a tablespoon of rum. Add about 25 g/1 oz/2 tablespoons of chopped almonds. Chill.

## Charlotte Russe

### SERVES 6-8

Line a lightly oiled mould with *madeleines* or *boudoirs* moistened slightly by dipping in black coffee mixed with dark rum or Cognac. Half fill with the same custard as for *Bavaroise au café*. Sprinkle with about 50 g/2 oz/4 tablespoons of chopped burnt almonds. Cover with a layer of moistened *boudoirs* or *madeleines* and pour the rest of the bavaroise cream over the top. Chill in the refrigerator for three or four hours. Unmould and serve with the above chocolate sauce.

## Mocha Soufflé

### SERVES 4

150 ml/¼ pint/⅔ cup milk
3 tablespoons ground coffee
25 g/1 oz/2 tablespoons butter
25 g/1 oz/¼ cup flour (scant measure)
25 g/1 oz/¼ cup bitter chocolate
2 tablespoons rum or coffee liqueur
3 egg yolks
4 egg whites

Bring the milk to the boil with the ground coffee. Leave for a few minutes and strain. Melt the butter. Stir in the flour and combine. Add the warm milk and stir until well blended. Add the chocolate, broken into small squares, and stir until melted. Remove from the heat. Drop in the . egg yolks, beating vigorously. At this point the mixture may be kept for a few hours. Just before serving, beat the egg whites with a pinch of salt until they form stiff peaks. Fold lightly into the mixture and turn into a well-buttered and sugared 1.5 l/2½ pint/1½ quarts soufflé dish. Cook in a preheated oven at 400°F, 200°C (gas 6) for about half an hour. Test with a skewer. If dry, serve immediately.

# $\mathscr{C}$OFFEE

## Pots de Crème à la Javanaise

### SERVES 6

600 ml/1 pint/2½ cups milk
3 tablespoons medium roast ground coffee
3 tablespoons sugar
3 egg yolks
1 whole egg

Bring the milk to the boil with the ground coffee and allow to infuse a few minutes. Strain. Stir in the sugar. In a bowl, lightly beat together the three egg yolks and one whole egg. Gradually pour in the milk, beating well. Pour the custard into ramekins. Place in a tray with water reaching up to two-thirds of the height of the pots. Bake in a preheated moderately slow oven 160°C, 325°F (gas 3) for about 45 minutes or until the cream has set.

For *Pots de Crème au Mocha*, melt 50 g/2 oz/½ cup chocolate, broken into pieces, in the milk at the same time as the sugar.

# Crème Saint-Honoré au Café

### SERVES 6–8

600 ml/1 pint/2½ cups milk
3–4 tablespoons ground coffee
175 g/6 oz/⅔ cup granulated sugar
5 eggs
65 g/2½ oz/½ cup sifted flour
1 tablespoon caster (superfine) sugar
2 tablespoons coffee liqueur or rum (optional)

Beat the egg yolks and 175 g/6 oz/⅔ cup sugar for two or three minutes until pale yellow and creamy. Add the flour and beat well. Bring the milk to the boil with the ground coffee. Stir and leave to infuse for a few minutes. Pour very gradually through a strainer over the egg yolk mixture, beating all the time until well blended. Pour into a heavy-bottomed saucepan and place over a moderate heat. Stir constantly with a wooden spoon until the mixture thickens. Use a whisk or electric beater if it becomes if it becomes lumpy. When it begins to boil continue to stir over very low heat for two to three minutes to allow the flour to cook. Be careful that the cream does not burn at the bottom of the pan. If you like, add two tablespoons of coffee liqueur or rum. Beat the egg whites with a pinch of salt until stiff. Add one tablespoon of caster (superfine) sugar and continue to beat until peaks are formed. Fold, a little at a time to begin with, into the hot cream. Chill in the refrigerator.

*Variations:* You may stir in 50 g/2 oz/½ cup of *pralin* (see method, *Mocha Praliné*, page 114) with the egg whites as a delicious alternative. For a Mocha version, beat 50 g/2 oz/½ cup of chocolate melted with the coffee liqueur, into the hot cream.

$\mathcal{C}$OFFEE

# Cakes

### Chestnut Gâteau
SERVES 6–8

500 g/1 lb chestnuts
600 ml/1 pint/2½ cups milk
3 tablespoons ground coffee
175 g/6 oz/⅔ cup sugar
3 egg whites
3 tablespoons sugar, for the caramel

With a sharp knife make an incision on the flat side of each chestnut. Put the chestnuts under the grill for 8–10 minutes and turn them over once. While they are still hot peel off the shell. Bring the milk to the boil with the ground coffee. Allow to infuse for a few minutes and strain. Cook the chestnuts in this milk with the sugar for about forty minutes. Put through a food mill or liquidizer. Make a caramel syrup by melting the three tablespoons of sugar and allowing it to turn brown. Add two tablespoons of water and stir until the caramel has melted. Pour into a mould (a round *savarin* tin will do well) and turn it around until the caramel has coated all the inside. Beat the egg whites until stiff and fold into the chestnuts. Pour into the coated mould. Place in a pan of hot water and cook forty-five minutes in a 160°C, 325°F (gas 2½) oven. Turn mould upside down on to a dish.
Serve cold garnished with whipped cream.

# Charlotte Malakoff au Café

SERVES 12 OR MORE

250 g/½ lb softened unsalted butter
175 g/6 oz/⅔ cup caster sugar
1 egg yolk
175 g/6 oz/⅔ cup coarsely ground almonds or
walnuts, or a mixture of both, or praliné hazelnuts
(see Mocha Praliné, page 114)
90 ml/3 fl oz/⅜ cup coffee made with 3
tablespoons ground coffee
400 ml/¾ pint/2 cups cream, whipping or a
mixture of single (light) and double (heavy)
40 sponge fingers
1 small glass rum, coffee liqueur or Cognac
300 ml/½ pint/1¼ cups milk
toasted split almonds

Cream butter and sugar for three or four minutes until soft. Beat in the
egg yolk and the coffee until a smooth cream. Stir in the ground
almonds or walnuts. Beat 400 ml/¾ pint/2 cups of whipping cream, or
300 ml/½ pint/1¼ cups of double (heavy) and 150 ml/¼ pint/⅔ cup of
single (light) cream, until stiff and fold into the almond and coffee
mixture.

Line a round cake tin – about 8 cm (3 in) high and 20 cm (8 in) in
diameter – with greaseproof paper. Dip the sponge fingers in the milk
mixed with the rum, Cognac or liqueur for a few seconds only. Turn
them over once and do not let them become saturated. Line the bottom
and sides of the tin with them. Turn half of the almond coffee cream into
the lined mould. Arrange a layer of the sponge fingers over it. Repeat
with another layer of cream and sponge fingers. Trim the tops of sponge
fingers lining the sides if necessary. Cover with greaseproof paper. Put
in the refrigerator for a few hours at least, preferably overnight, before
serving. The cream must be chilled firm.

Remove the greaseproof paper. Run a knife around the inside of the
mould and turn the dessert out on to a serving dish. Peel the greaseproof
paper from the top and return to the refrigerator until serving time. Decorate with toasted split almonds, and serve with whipped cream.

## Diplomate Mocha Praliné

This creamy cake has been my father's favourite ever since I can remember. My mother made it for him every year on his birthday. When I was in Cairo a few years ago, I found it in a book of cake photographs in a little pastry shop near our old home. It is still a popular party cake there. The photograph must have been at least forty years old. It shows the cake exactly as I make it.

100 g/4 oz/1 cup blanched hazelnuts
100 g/4 oz/½ cup + 3 tablespoons caster
(superfine) sugar
600 ml/1 pint/2½ cups double (heavy) cream
1 heaped tablespoon instant coffee, or more to taste
3 packets *boudoirs* (16 x 3 biscuits (cookies))
*Café au lait*, or weak black coffee to dip the
biscuits (cookies) in

First make a *pralin* with the hazelnuts, keeping a few whole caramelized hazelnuts to decorate.

To make the *pralin:* Toast 100 g/4 oz/1 cup hazelnuts in a dry frying pan (skillet), shaking the pan (skillet) so that they are slightly browned all over. Add 100 g/4 oz/½ cup sugar and stir until the sugar is melted and brown. Stir so that the hazelnuts are covered with liquid caramel. Pour on to an oiled baking tray and let it cool. When it is hard and brittle, grind in a food processor.

Next, beat the double (heavy) cream. Add three tablespoons of sugar and one tablespoon or more of instant coffee dissolved in a tablespoon of warm milk. Moisten the *boudoirs* by dipping them a few seconds in *café au lait* or weak black coffee. Do not let them soak up too much liquid or they will become soggy. Start by putting a layer of *boudoirs* in a round or square mould with a loose base or detachable sides. Spread with a layer of cream and sprinkle with a little *pralin*. Repeat the layers until all the *boudoirs* are used up, ending with a good layer of cream. Lift out the *diplomate* from the base or remove the sides of the mould. Spread a little of the coffee cream around the sides. Sprinkle all over the *pralin* and place the whole caramelized nuts on the top of the gâteau.

This cake freezes very well. Just out of the freezer it is like a *semifreddo* ice cream.

## Walnut and Coffee Cake

### SERVES 8

4 eggs, separated
100 g/4 oz/1 cup icing (confectioner's) sugar
175 g/6 oz/1½ cups walnuts, coarsely chopped
1 tablespoon powdered drinking chocolate
1 tablespoon pulverized ground coffee
1 tablespoon fine breadcrumbs

Cream the egg yolks and sugar. Add breadcrumbs, coffee and chocolate powder and combine thoroughly. Add the walnuts and mix well. Gently fold in the stiffly beaten egg whites and pour into a cake tin (about 20 cm, 8 in diameter) which has been greased with butter and dusted with flour. Bake in a preheated 180°C, 350°F (gas 4) oven for forty-five minutes. When the cake is cool, turn out and spread with a butter cream made with:

100 g/4 oz/½ cup unsalted butter
100 g/4 oz/1 cup icing (confectioner's) sugar
1 egg yolk
2 tablespoons very strong coffee, made by pouring
3 tablespoons of boiling water over a
heaped tablespoon of ground coffee and straining.

Cream the butter and sugar. Add
the egg yolk and the coffee,
and beat well to a smooth cream.

# $\mathcal{C}$ OFFEE

## Ricotta al Caffé

A very simple and delicious custom in Italy is to serve ricotta with bowls of ground coffee and sugar and a bottle of rum for everyone to help themselves and mix in as much as they please. On the other hand it is better to make the mixture in advance and to allow the coffee to infuse for an hour at least before serving. For four to six people mix 500 g/1 lb ricotta with six tablespoons of caster (superfine) sugar and four tablespoons medium or dark roast pulverized (as for Turkish) coffee. Pass the rum around.

## Tiramisu
This Italian dessert has become popular around the world
in the last decade.

SERVES 8

4 tablespoons of rum
100 ml/4 fl oz/½ cup strong black coffee
16–20 sponge (lady) fingers
400 g/14 oz mascarpone
2 medium eggs, separated
4 tablespoons icing (confectioner's) sugar
75–100 g/3–4 oz/¾ –1 cup bitter chocolate

Mix two tablespoons of rum with the coffee. Dip the sponge (lady) fingers in briefly and arrange them in a shallow serving dish. Pour over any remaining coffee but not so much that the sponge becomes soggy. Beat the mascarpone with the egg yolks, icing (confectioner's) sugar and the remaining rum. Whisk the egg whites until stiff and fold them in, then spread the mixture over the sponge (lady) fingers. Pulverize the chocolate in a food processor and sprinkle over the top. Cover with clingfilm (plastic wrap) and refrigerate overnight.

ACKNOWLEDGEMENTS

I wish to thank all the friends who have talked to me about coffee, and the many people in the specialist coffee trade who have given me their views and precious information. My warmest thanks are for my brother Zaki who helped me with his ready and generous advice for the first edition of this book. I thought of him often as I worked on the new one. I have special thanks for Tony Santos, for his early enthusiasm for the project, and for Suzette Macedo, for access to Uker's *All About Coffee*. The book was published in New York in 1922 by the Tea and Coffee Trade Journal of which William H. Ukers was the long-time editor. It was my constant companion throughout my early research. For information about coffee I gratefully acknowledge the help of Kerry Muir of the International Coffee Organisation, Mr Sylvio Lima of the Brazilian Coffee Institute, Mr Arl of Appleton, Machin and Smiles, and in particular the late George Markus of the Markus Coffee Co. Ltd in Connaught Street and his daughter Mari who were so generous. I am especially indebted to Mr Pablo Dubois of the International Coffee Organisation and Marianne Bradnock, their librarian, for making available a number of books and publications, trade journals and articles and for talking to me. Most important and valuable among the books was Philippe Jobin's monumental *Les Cafés Produits dans le Monde*.

# Index

# Coffee –
## Showing the major producing countries of the world.

Hawaii

Mexico

Guatemala

El Salvador

Nicaragua

Costa Rica

Panama

Colombia

Ecuador

Peru

Bolivia

Cuba

Jamaica / Haiti

Honduras

Puerto Rico

Dominica

Venezuela

Trinidad

Guyana

Brazil

Ivory Coast

Togo

Gabon

Congo

Zaire

Angola

etimes debt collectors, sometimes private soldiers, sometimes bouncers.
ese are dependable yakuza that will give their lives for the Yakuza Clan.
veryone being harassed by the real yakuza, we bring good news!

## The Clone Yakuza Y-12 has finally rolled out!
### We've realized our three goals: Tasty, Fast, and Cheap!!!

r company holds the patent to a proprietary program that teaches them
rious skills and karate. Even if they're being pumped full of lead or having
eir fingers cut off by their master, they will follow orders to the death. Most
ective when used in teams of a few to several dozen.
der now! Buy one, get one free!

rammed to use handguns, katana, man-catcher pitchforks, blackjack sticks,
mic battle-axes, riot shock nunchuks, rifles, and RPGs right out of the box!

Clone Yakuza are not robots. They are cloned humans with living brains and bio-blood
engineered via biotechnology. They are programmed to have a lifespan of 3 years.

# NINJA SLAYER Volume 1
## ~MACHINE OF VENGEANCE~

A Vertical Comics Edition

Translation: Christian Storms and HCL
Original Production: Keiran O'Leary
Production: Grace Lu

© 2012 NINJ@ ENTERTAINMENT
© Yuki YOGO 2013    © Yoshiaki TABATA 2013
Edited by KADOKAWA SHOTEN
First published in Japan in 2013 by KADOKAWA CORPORATION, Tokyo.
English translation rights arranged with KADOKAWA CORPORATION, Tokyo
through TUTTLE-MORI AGENCY, INC., Tokyo.

Published by Vertical Comics, an imprint of Vertical, Inc., New York

Originally published in Japanese as *Ninja Sureiyaa~Mashin Obu Venjensu~* by Kado
*Ninja Sureiyaa* first serialized in *Comptiq*, Kadokawa, 2013-

*Ninja Slayer* was created based on contents from the original *Ninja Slayer* novels
some details, including time periods, the order of events, and character settings
been changed with the consent of the original authors.

This is a work of fiction.

ISBN: 978-1-941220-93-1

Manufactured in Canada

First Edition

Vertical, Inc.
451 Park Avenue South
7th Floor
New York, NY 10016
www.vertical-inc.com

Vertical books are distributed through Penguin-Random House Publisher Servi

# Y-12

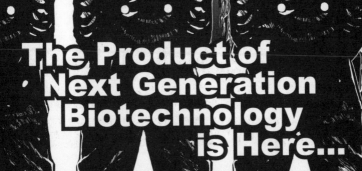

The Product of
Next Generation
Biotechnology
is Here...

SPECTACULAR PHOTO!
It's not a fish.
TAMA SPORTS
150 YEN
The MAGURO ZEPPELIN
GETS MAD!
Super Mad! GRRRRR!!!
EXPLOSIONS atop buildings!
KITTY KI
In Neo Saitama, String of W
Pandemonium at the destroye
shrapnel everyw
eople runnin
despair an

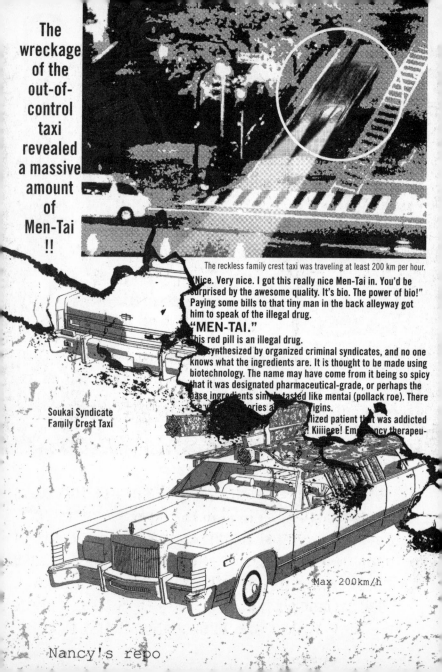

# The wreckage of the out-of-control taxi revealed a massive amount of Men-Tai !!

The reckless family crest taxi was traveling at least 200 km per hour.

"Nice. Very nice. I got this really nice Men-Tai in. You'd be surprised by the awesome quality. It's bio. The power of bio!" Paying some bills to that tiny man in the back alleyway got him to speak of the illegal drug.

## "MEN-TAI."

This red pill is an illegal drug.

...synthesized by organized criminal syndicates, and no one knows what the ingredients are. It is thought to be made using biotechnology. The name may have come from it being so spicy that it was designated pharmaceutical-grade, or perhaps the base ingredients simply tasted like mentai (pollack roe). There are v... ...ories a... ...igins.

...lized patient th t was addicted ...l Kiiiieee! Eme ncy therapeu-

Soukai Syndicate
Family Crest Taxi

Max 200km/h

Nancy's repo

It's finally come this far!

# "BLACK MARKET TRADING OF MEN-TAI IN NEO SAITAMA"

## Death-defying report!

To our readers:
Even hundreds of years after the era of Tokugawa Edo, this high-tech land in the Far East continues to give the utmost importance to the concepts of "honor" and "courtesy"—to be humble and to abase oneself while paying others the highest respect. harmony is the top priority. Loser drug addicts drug dealers are no exception to this rule.

AND SET THE DOJO ON FIRE!

TEAM UP WITH EARTH-QUAKE

ヨロコンデ！

WITH PLEASURE!

**Neo-Yakuza For Sale: END**

NOT BAD, YOROSHI-SAN.

HOW DO YOU LIKE THAT LAOMOTO-SAN?!

OUR NEW CLONE YAKUZA Y-12 FROM YOROSHISAN PHARMA-CEUTICALS!

THE Y-12 IS INVINCIBLE!

WHETHER FACING OFF WITH COPS OR SUMO WRESTLERS, THE RESULTS ARE THE SAME!

THANK YOU, MOST KIND OF YOU!

Laomoto Khan lets out a guffaw.

Thus boasts the Yoroshi-san sales-man.

# RELEASE ME!

With that cry, a vicious Mexican lion

ap-pears from the Ukiyoe Geisha Gate!

Not even fifty ordinary men can kill him !!!

How-ever ...

These serialized episodes don't occur in chronological order. Why, you ask? There is a universal inevitability behind it, but it's a pain in the ass to explain, so I won't. What I'm trying to say is, just read the current episode if you're confused. If you're still worried, read it again. Even better, just buy the book. That's what I've heard, at least.

NJSLYR 10/14/2012

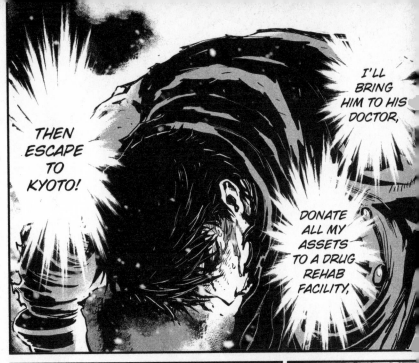

I'LL BRING HIM TO HIS DOCTOR,

THEN ESCAPE TO KYOTO!

DONATE ALL MY ASSETS TO A DRUG REHAB FACILITY,

I'M GONNA TURN MY LIFE AROUND!

BECOME A BUDDHIST IN KYOTO!

SOB

STUDY ZEN AND BECOME A MONK.

NO, ACTUALLY, HIS EYES ARE A HUNDRED TIMES SCARIER!

THOSE EYES... THE SAME FIERCE EYES AS THE DEMON FROM LAST NIGHT.

OF COURSE! WITH PLEASURE!

A scared-shitless quick reply!

I'LL FILL YOU IN LATER! JUST DO AS I SAY!

UH... SURE.

HUH?

LADY LUCK IS ON OUR S-SIDE AFTER ALL!

HUH?

SHUT UP! STOP RIGHT THERE!

BOSS?

BRRT F F F F F F BRRT BRRT

ZWISH

PLEASE LET ME LIVE. DON'T DO IT.

MUTTER

I'LL TAKE YOU. I'M VERY SORRY.

WHISPER

WHISPER

.......
.......

BRUMMMM

WH-
WHERE
...

...
AM I
...?

SHAKE  SHAKE

OLD
TOKYO

BAY
...

SHIVER

His
hellish
glare
froze
Smith's
spine!

TAKE ME...
TO MY
BACK-
ALLEY
DOCTOR
...

TAKE
ME
NOW
...

WHAT A LET-DOWN.

I'LL JUST CHECK HIS POCKETS...

TATTERS

WAS HE WRAPPED IN A BAMBOO MAT AND THROWN IN THE RIVER AS PUNISHMENT?

DID HE WASH OUT TO SEA FROM THE RIVER?

ZLOSH

The hand that gripped his was as powerful as a vise!

CLUTCH

WHAT THE FUCK?!

AIEE?!

A SURVI-VOR?

AND SOMEONE IS CLINGING TO IT.

NO. SOME KIND OF WRECKAGE.

A RAFT?

A JUNKED BOAT?

SMELLS LIKE MONEY.

...

WHAT DO YOU WANT TO DO? IT'S A PERSON.

VROOM

*Koban: a flat gold ingot.

HE MIGHT HAVE A KOBAN* IN HIS POCKET!

IT'S DO-OR-DIE FOR OUR CLAN!

OUR SHAKEN-UP FAMILY NEEDS TO SEE THEIR LEADER'S DECISIVENESS RIGHT NOW.

More than anything else, the previous evening's events were a major ordeal for the clan.

JERMAINE AND DIVO STILL HAVEN'T WOKEN UP FROM NRS (NINJA REALITY SHOCK)... THEY'RE IN CRITICAL CONDITION.

RUMORS MIGHT'VE ALREADY SPREAD AMONG THE SHARP-EARED FISHERMEN.

ANY BOAT WILL DO... EVEN ONE ALREADY UNDER OUR PROTECTION.

BOSS! OVER THERE!

WHAZ-ZUP?

IF WE LET GUYS MESS WITH US, WE'RE DONE FOR!

WE GOTTA PLAY UP OUR GANG'S VICIOUS-NESS TO THE WHOLE AREA!

WE'LL PICK A FIGHT, SURROUND 'EM, AND CLUB 'EM.

Those boys sure get up early!

The Yokohama Ropeway Clan.

NINJA SLAYER-SAN...!

The demon gargoyle zeppelin morphed into a ball of fire

and slowly tumbled towards the Tama River.

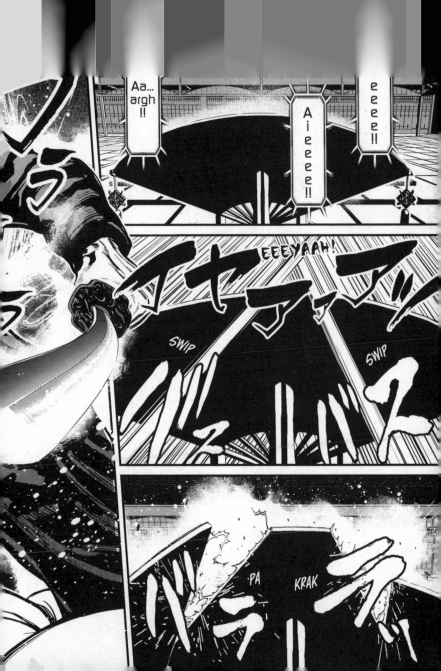

Then, like fireworks...

Reduced to a fireball, Cloud Buster charts a random, crazed course through the night sky!

IS BLOWN

NAMU AMIDA BUTSU!

'TIL KINGDOM COME.

KAPOOOOOW

the demon gargoyle zeppelin!

WHOOOOO

GREAT HEAVENS!!

KRAK

KA

KRUNCH

I-IN-DUS-TRY!

WWOOSH

KASHING

Sparks fly!

WHY ?!

IT'S A WEAPON OF MODERN CIVILIZATION!

THE ELECTRIC SHOCK MUST HAVE PASSED THROUGH HIM!

But Ninja Slayer takes no heed!

# BLOOD-LUST.

LIKE THAT... BWA HA HA HA ...

YOU'LL NEVER LAG BEHIND A CRANE FLY LIKE THAT.

WITH MY ALPHA SOURCE KARATE

A PETTY CLAN WITH PETTY KARATE AND A PETTY COURT RANK!

THAT LESSER NINJA FROM THE WASP CLAN...

TRULY, MERE INSECTS IN THE KARMIC CYCLE OF LIFE ...

NARAKU!!

NNG

NNG

NNG

NGK

I CAN STILL GO ON ...

I WILL DO IT.

NGK

STAND DOWN.

NNG

Fujikido: Ninja Slayer's real name.

FUJI-KIDO.

GAH

HA HA HA HA HA

SILENCE, YOU DAMN GHOUL...

I HAD MUCH HIGHER ASPIRATIONS FOR YOU.

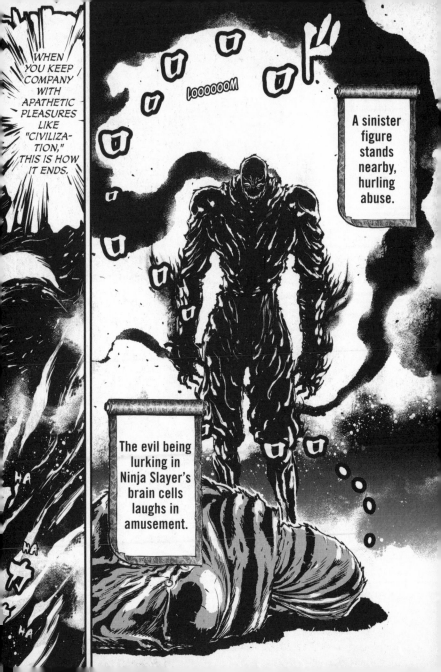

Like a bio-starfish sunk into the abyssal plain

Ninja Slayer's murky *mano-vijnana* consciousness

floats helplessly amid the neuron darkness.

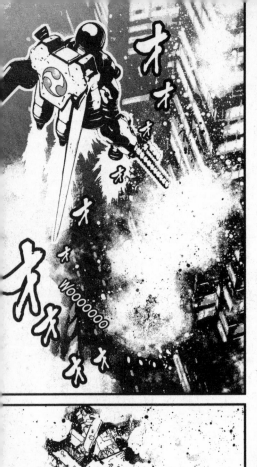

WOOOOOOO

**NAKED SUSHI CHEFS**

GORGEOUS!

Laomoto laughs merrily.

His delight affects the blonde courtesans, causing them to simultaneously climax.

Thumbs up

HE'S DONE, HUZZAH!!!!!

# MACHINE OF VENGEANCE #4

Hit and away !!

SOON AFTER ...

Ninja Slayer leaps back out of the way!

CLUTCH

SHRK

But there's no convenient building right behind him!

Without a moment's delay, the laser beams are already tracking his movements!

NGH ....!

But then!

BOOOM

LEAP

KAR

Ninja Slayer does a series of back hand-springs!

FWIP

FWIP

FWIP

By the skin of his teeth

FWIP

NAY!

A jitte truncheon?

BEEET
BEEET
BEEET
BEEET

AARGH!

MORE TECHNOLOGY FROM OMURA INDUSTRIES!

KRAAAKLE

ZISSH

BAM

Ninja Slayer's internal organs will be fried, and he will **perish!**

SMOLDER

Ninja or not, if hit repeatedly by that weapon,

EEYAAAH! EEYAAAH! EEYAAAH! EEYAAAH!

There's no end in sight to his lightning-fast momentum.

How many dozens, how many hundreds of suriken has he thrown?

VWOOOSH

Something ejects and homes in fast, like a humming-bird.

At last, combustion!

BOOOOM

But just then...!

MY PLEA- SURE.

ROGER.

FWIP

FWIP

FWIP

FWIP

YEEART!

AIEEE!!

Do what you want. Just kill the enemy!

UH, NO, I MEAN, NOT AS FORMAL BUSINESS ...

ZMM ZMM

LAO- MOTO- SAN!

I'D LIKE TO TAKE THIS CHANCE TO PRESENT OUR COMPANY'S NINJA CAPABILITIES.

BA-SHING

KRING

KRING KRING

WHAT? WHAT ON EARTH?

RATTLE

カ゛ッ

AIEEEEE!

Ninja Slayer's suriken aren't mere slingshot pebbles, mind you.

カ゛ッ

RATTLE

OMURA

カ゛ッ

RATTLE

AIEE!

Is he beyond your control, Omura-san?

With all that firepower onboard, you can't defeat a single rogue ninja?

Are you going to allow his counter-attack?

The optical laser scanner hunts down Ninja Slayer.

BWOOSH

BWOOSH

A-LAS!

BWOOSH

BWOOSH

The Bubu-jima soars high above.

What will Ninja Slayer do?

While ignoring the monitor,

CLUTCH

WELL, SHOW ME HOW YOUR LITTLE TOY WORKS.

DO YOUR BEST TO ENTERTAIN ME.

Absolutely. You're absolutely right!

UNG

GAAAH

Laomoto gobbles up two pieces of organic fatty tuna sushi at once.

GAAAH

Hmm, well done.

WE HAVE DETECTED THE PRESENCE OF THE TARGETED NINJA.

I AM THRILLED TO SO QUICKLY PRESENT TO YOU THE OVERWHELMING FIREPOWER

OF OUR COMPANY'S BATTLE DEMON GARGOYLE AIRSHIP, THE BUBUJIMA.

Domo, Lao-moto-san.

BOW

Note the Omura Industries emblem embossed on his helmet.

Captain Kinjima here.

THE OMURA INDUSTRIES COMPANY SONG:
TO THE UTMOST POWER
STRONG IN EVERY RESPECT
WE ARE EQUAL
AS MACHINES IN THIS WORLD

AS COGS IN THE WHEEL, WE DO OUR BEST.
AS COGS IN THE WHEEL, LET'S WORK
LET'S BEGIN THIS HAPPY DAY
NOW, FEEL ONE WITH THE MACHINE
WE TRULY HAVE NO DOUBTS

SIGNIFICANT OMURA
OUR OMURA
TREMENDOUS OMURA
TRUE TO ITS REPUTATION, OMURA

Omura Industries, an underworld mega-corporation, has a monopoly in Japan's heavy industries field.

Their connection with the Soukai Syndicate runs very deep. They're thick as thieves!

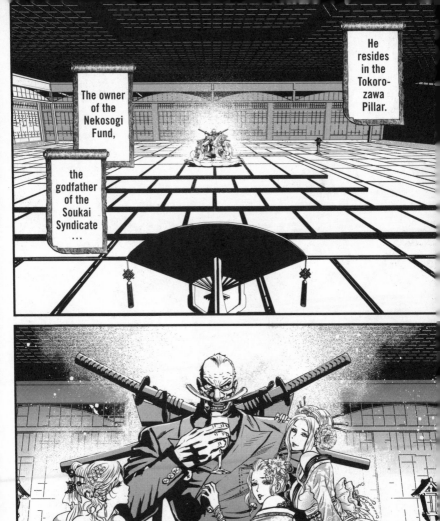

The owner of the Nekosogi Fund,

the godfather of the Soukai Syndicate…

He resides in the Tokorozawa Pillar.

**LAOMOTO KHAN**
ラオモト・カン

# The Tokorozawa Pillar Castle Tower

However, only the ruling class is allowed to enjoy the beauty of the nightscape from a high vantage point.

Namely, men like *him*.

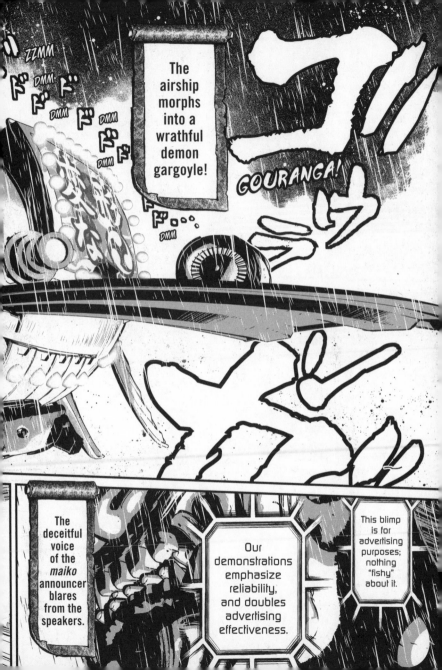

The airship morphs into a wrathful demon gargoyle!

*ZZMM*

*GOURANGA!*

The deceitful voice of the *maiko* announcer blares from the speakers.

Our demonstrations emphasize reliability, and doubles advertising effectiveness.

This blimp is for advertising purposes; nothing "fishy" about it.

and launched this weapon which is camouflaged as a Maguro Zeppelin!

The enemy air control center quickly responded to Arson's distress call,

In fact, this counter-ninja airship was dispatched by the Soukai Syndicate.

RRRUMBLE

KRASH

RURR

ZWIP

ZWIP

Behold!

AND TRANS-FORMS!

KASHANK

KASHANK

The tuna unfurls its exterior cladding,

GRANK

RURR

RURR

RURR

The Maguro Zeppelin sends out laser beams.

Its target: Ninja Slayer !!

KROOOM

# MACHINE OF VENGEANCE #3

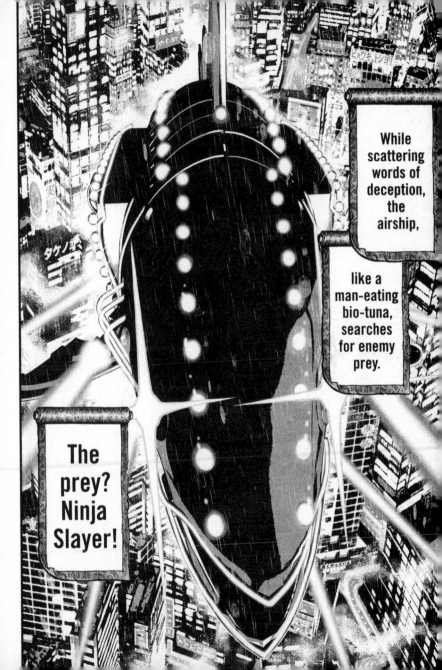

FLASH

He simply stares down with blank eyes that suggest he's seen this sort of carnage many times before.

ROLL

ゴロ...

ZPATT

チオ

ド

WOOOO

オ

Arson's headless body

Then ...

glistens mysteriously in the light ...

OOOOOO

A hellish thrusting chop

pierces right through Arson's torso...

NAMU AMIDA BUTSU

YOU'RE
...
DONE
FOR,
TOO...

AHK

HORRRK

THEN
...,
AND
THEN
...

STRONGER NINJA WARRIORS WILL...

EVEN IF YOU AVOID THEM,

RESCUE IS ALREADY HEADING THIS WAY
...

TOTTER

COULD THE RUMOR BE TRUE ...?

KRIK

KRAK

KLATTER

KLATTER

OOF ...

ZSSH

ZSSH

ALL ON YOUR OWN ?!

ARE YOU SERIOUSLY TRYING TO ANNIHILATE US SOUKAI NINJA ?!

ARE YOU ...

DEAD

SERIOUS.

Ninja Slayer

RUMBLE

assumes a *jiu-jitsu* stance.

WHOOMM

GULP

inscribed in a fear-instilling font!

Neon light illuminates two kanji characters: *nin* (ninja) and *satsu* (slayer)

He handed down a death sentence in a voice like the Grim Reaper himself!

Thus it is written in the Records of Ancient Matters.

It is simply proper ninja etiquette.

The exchange of courtesies must not be neglected.

HMM...

I NEVER BELIEVED YOU TRULY EXISTED.

SHFF

I FIGURED YOU WERE JUST A CONVENIENT FICTION INVENTED BY LOSERS TO EVADE RESPONSIBILITY.

CLENCH

SINCE I'M GOING TO BREAK YOUR KARATE AND SEND YOU OFF TO HELL.

BE AT EASE.

NO NEED TO CONSIDER FACTS VERSUS FICTION,

YOU DARE UTTER SUCH WORDS?

WHAT ...?

NINJA SLAYER, YOU SAY?

I AM ARSON.

DOMO, NINJA SLAYER-SAN.

URK

SHFF

However ...

Of course, after the pleasantries are dealt with, a gruesome battle to the death will follow.

When you first lay eyes on such a scene, you might find it discomfiting.

suriken throwing stars!

The special throwing weapon of a ninja:

A cross-shaped mass of steel protrudes from each of their skulls.

AND THREW STARS WITH PEERLESS ACCURACY IN A SPLIT SECOND, MUST BE A—

THIS MAN...

WHO SURVIVED A BARRAGE OF BULLETS

GASP

CLAP

GOURANGA!

MACHINE OF VENGEANCE #2

VROOOOM

GRIPP

HEY.

THIS IS THE WRONG ROUTE,

IDIOT.

SORRY, SIR.

WHAT?

YOU'RE NOT GOING TO THE TOKORO-ZAWA PILLAR.

BUT THIS WILL GET YOU WHERE YOU'RE GOING.

WHAT DID YOU SAY?

KLNK

MY PLEA-SURE.

TAKE ME TO THE TOKORO-ZAWA PILLAR.

AT YOUR SER-VICE.

VROOOOM

I SEE.

YES, SIR.

INDEED, SIR. KAMEJI-SAN RETIRED.

DID YOU CHANGE SHIFTS? YOU'RE NOT THE SAME PERSON AS LAST WEEK.

DRI-VER...

NINJA ...
NINJA ...
WITH ONE PUNCH THEY BURST INTO FLAMES ...
ONLY A NINJA COULD PERFORM SUCH A TRICK...!
ONLY A TRUE NINJA POSSESSES SUCH TECHNIQUES!

AN...

DRE?

WIND
PRES-
SURE
BLAST!

SWOOSH

HALT

WIND
PRES-
SURE
BLAST!

HALT

ZWUM

HAA
HAA
!

HEE
HEE HEE!
ANDRE!
GO EASY
ON HIM!

HYOK

HYOK HYOK

YOU
KNOW HE'S
FREAKIN'
OUT ON
THE
INSIDE!

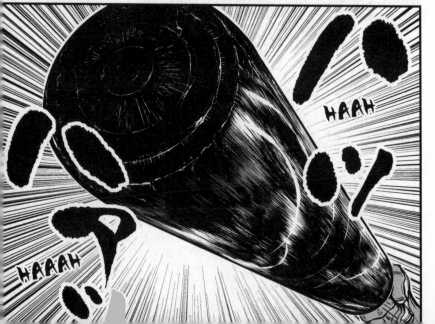

THIS IS BULL-SHIT!

YOU FUCKIN' BAS-TARDS!

TOTAL BULL-SHIT!

So scary!

Any law-abiding Neo Saitama citizen would surely piss his pants!

HEH HEH HEH ...

SWIP

Super scary!

I'LL KILL YOU!

BONE-HEADS!

WE'RE RAISING THE WHOLESALE PRICE,

DUE TO THE RUSSIAN SUPPLIER AND RUBLE EXCHANGE RATE.

THE MEN-TAI PRICE...

WHAT'S THIS ALL ABOUT, HUH?

Smith screams out some intimidating yakuza slang!

How scary!

DON'T YOU DARE FUCK WITH US

# DOMO! WE ARE TERRIBLY SORRY!

BOW BOW BOW BOW

DOMO.

...!

\* Domo: Greetings

Despite the calm-before-the-storm air of imminent battle, yakuza and ninja alike prioritize proper greetings.

AGING

ILLNESS

YOROSHISAN

Buddha shuns such deeds! The devil's research!

These yakuza clones share a syngeneic genotype created by Yoroshisan Pharmaceuticals.

...

PUNCTU- ALITY IS A JAPANESE VIRTUE, AIN'T IT?

YOU'RE LATE.

DAFUQ
?
YAKUZA
CLONES
?

PTOO

...

Reports of their practical use had swept the criminal world, but this was their first time seeing them in action.

GULP

The Black yakuza are alarmed.

MURMUR

MURMUR

MURMUR

YROOOM

ウーゴ

ウーゴ

オ

オ

オ

オ

WHOOOOO

These "family crest" taxis are the faithful, preferred means of transport for a certain yakuza clan.

SKREEK-

キ

キ

キ

キ

FUCK!

ゴ

KOFF

ゴ

KOFF

KOFF

....!

The Black yakuza gasp.

ジャ

ジャ

CHAK

CHAK

サリ

ZHFF

サリ

ZHFF

Tire smoke from a drifting car!

A blinding light!

Then ...

FLASH

BRUMM

BRUMM

VRUMMM

It's a "family crest" taxi!

BRUMM

BRUMM

BRUMM

BRUMM

BRUMM

SKREE

SKREEK

These club-gripping,

rope-wielding,

jet-ski straddling, tuna-boat-raiding bad boys are...

a cold-blooded, brutal criminal mob!

Giving off an unusually dangerous vibe,

MY PATIENCE IS WEARIN' DANGEROUSLY THIN.

HE'S LATE...

The name of this band of brothers is...

the Black yakuza waited, on alert.

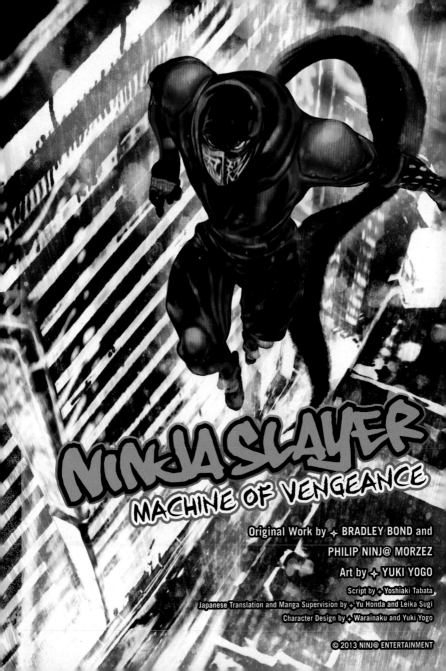

# NINJA SLAYER

## MACHINE OF VENGEANCE

Original Work by ✦ **BRADLEY BOND** and

**PHILIP NINJ@ MORZEZ**

Art by ✦ **YUKI YOGO**

Script by ✦ Yoshiaki Tabata

Japanese Translation and Manga Supervision by ✦ Yu Honda and Leika Sugi

Character Design by ✦ Warainaku and Yuki Yogo

One was a yakuza.

NAMU AMIDA BUTSU

Another yakuza.

* Praise the Buddha

The man's arms are fouled with blood, the blood of the five slain men beside him.

NAMU AMIDA BUTSU

NAMU AMIDA BUTSU

Yakuza!

Yakuza!

Yet the final man was...

*BOOM*

A TRUE NINJA !!

A NINJA !!!

NAMU AMIDA BUTSU

# CONTENTS

## MACHINE OF VENGEANCE